CONTENTS

HARCOURT

Math

Success for English Language Learners ESOL/ESL

Grade 4

Harcourt

Orlando Austin Chicago New York Toronto London San Diego

Visit *The Learning Site!*
www.harcourtschool.com

Printed in the United States of America

ISBN 0-15-336546-3

1 2 3 4 5 6 7 8 9 10 021 10 09 08 07 06 05 04 03

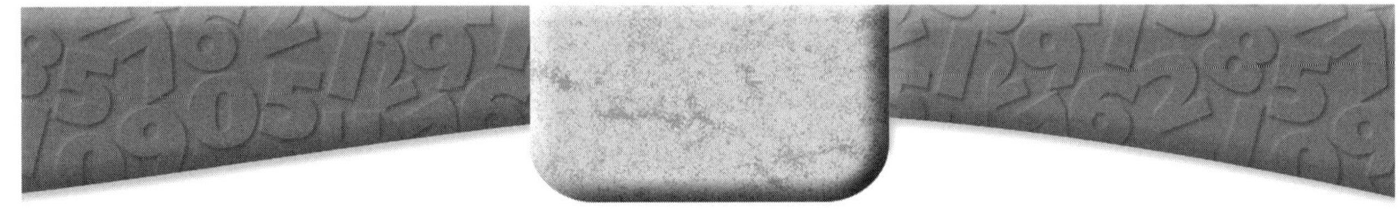

Strategies for Success

Throughout the United States, students with limited English proficiency and their teachers face daily challenges in the classroom. One of the greatest challenges for students is learning subjects taught in a language they have not yet mastered. The challenge for teachers is providing instruction that students clearly understand. Academic instruction designed especially for the English language learner (ELL) meets those challenges. These strategies do not lower standards or change academic expectations for English language learners. Instead, they modify instruction to meet students' diverse linguistic and cultural needs. Through these strategies, students gain equal access to the curriculum, and they experience academic success.

Rationale and Research

Research has shown that five to seven years of appropriate instruction are needed to acquire academic proficiency in a second language (Krashen, 1982). Postponing content instruction until students gain full mastery of English would be unreasonable and a disservice to these students. Educators realize that with carefully planned lessons and the use of a variety of research-based practices designed to meet the needs of ELLs, students can meet content standards *while* demonstrating growth in English language proficiency.

Stages of English-Language Acquisition

Proficiency Level: BEGINNER

PRE-PRODUCTION

Listening/Speaking

- associate utterances with meanings
- use unanalyzed phrases sporadically
- may need to use native language to demonstrate comprehension
- respond nonverbally or with one or two words and short phrases
- participate in songs, chants, and rhymes

Reading

- decode but have difficulty with English phonological awareness
- comprehend simple content
- begin to read single words and short phrases

Writing

- copy, label, and list
- write familiar words and phrases

EARLY PRODUCTION

Listening/Speaking

- begin to model verb tenses, such as present participles
- ask and answer simple questions about familiar concepts
- participate in face-to-face conversations with peers
- begin to self-check and self-correct

Reading

- comprehend and recall main ideas of a simple story or other content
- improve pronunciation and phonological awareness
- read student generated text

Writing

- use graphic organizers and writing frames
- write simple questions and answers

Proficiency Level: **INTERMEDIATE**

SPEECH EMERGENCE

Listening/Speaking

- express thoughts and use original language
- use complete simple sentences
- produce sustained conversation

Reading

- interact with a variety of print
- use writing for a variety of purposes

Writing

- transfer reading and oral language to writing
- write for a variety of purposes
- participate fully in editing

INTERMEDIATE FLUENCY

Listening/Speaking

- use the listening process to improve comprehension and oral skills
- clarify, distinguish, and evaluate ideas and responses
- demonstrate adequate pronunciation and grammar usage

Reading

- use a variety of reading strategies
- use various study skills

Writing

- use extended written production in all content areas
- use adjectives, adverbs, and figurative language in writing

Proficiency Level: **ADVANCED**

ADVANCED FLUENCY

Listening/Speaking

- create, clarify, critique, and evaluate ideas and responses
- comprehend concrete and abstract topics and concepts
- use effortless, fluent speech

Reading

- use graphophonic cues, syntax, context, and prior knowledge to make meaning
- read grade-level materials with limited difficulty

Writing

- use graphophonic cues, syntax, context, and prior knowledge to create meaning
- write to meet social needs and academic demands

Teaching Strategies

Language is learned in a variety of ways, but experience and time are important factors that foster proficiency. To acquire a second language, students must receive large amounts of *comprehensible input* (Krashen, 1982). Comprehensible input describes the understandable and meaningful language directed toward learners acquiring a second language. Language and the delivery of concepts are either decontextualized (with few clues) or contextualized (rich with clues). Traditional instruction has been very decontextualized, but English language learners rely on contextualized instruction and materials for comprehensible input (Cummins, 1994). Characteristics of comprehensible input include the following:

- Focus on communicating a meaningful message rather than on language forms
- Frequent use of concrete contextual referents, such as visuals, manipulatives, and graphics
- Acceptance of primary language use by the learner
- Minimal overt correction by the instructor
- Establishment of positive and motivating learning environments.

Language learning is developmental. When students receive comprehensible input, they progress through predictable levels of language proficiency. Students at various proficiency levels have specific characteristics and need different instructional strategies. The lesson focus also changes at different proficiency levels.

Teaching Strategies: BEGINNER

• Provide opportunities for purposeful listening and speaking • Surround students with environmental print • Use rhymes, chants, songs, and games • Group students by mixed language ability and provide for paired learning • Use students' prior knowledge • Address all learning modalities • Provide a low-anxiety environment • Ask questions that can be answered with one- or two- word responses	• Incorporate both cooperative and collaborative group opportunities • Use non-verbal role-playing • Incorporate visual aids, realia, or manipulatives when possible • Use multisensory lessons when introducing new information • Provide opportunities to apply vocabulary • Write key points and directions on board or chart

Teaching Strategies: INTERMEDIATE

- Provide opportunities for listening comprehension with contextual support
- Ask questions requiring yes/no, either/or, and listing responses
- Ask questions that require group discussion responses
- Have students label and/or categorize visuals or manipulatives
- Use patterned or predictable text
- Provide structure for writing and reading
- Incorporate shared reading and writing lessons
- Have students use numerical symbols
- Have students use a variety of graphic organizers
- Review frequently to reinforce learning
- Provide notes or outlines and use journal writing for new information
- Ask open-ended questions, and encourage students to describe, restate, and expand language
- Model mathematical concepts and conduct guided lessons using concrete models
- Use visuals, role-playing, and skits to promote conceptual learning
- Focus on vocabulary/concept development
- Provide a variety of texts (genres and levels) for independent reading and concept attainment
- Encourage students to compare and contrast mathematical concepts

Teaching Strategies: ADVANCED

- Provide structure for discussions and assignments
- Guide use of reference material for research and independent work
- Provide opportunities for students to create oral and written narratives
- Provide a variety of realistic writing and speaking experiences
- Encourage creative expression
- Focus on sustained vocabulary/concept development
- Continue direct, explicit skill instruction
- Provide opportunities for students to support and defend positions or opinions
- Model and guide students in predicting outcomes
- Provide age-appropriate reading and writing materials
- Continue ongoing language development through integrated language arts and content-area activities

Scaffolding Principles and Strategies

To encourage students to develop cognition, handle complex language tasks, and take risks, use scaffolding strategies to organize instruction. The lesson format and strategies in this book incorporate the following scaffolding principles and strategies.

Comprehensible Input

Use rich context to introduce vocabulary and concepts. Speak slowly and enunciate words exactly. Avoid the use of idioms and colloquialisms. Use gestures, facial expressions and dramatization. Use visuals such as realia, pictures, and graphic organizers.

Modeling

Use explicit instructions. Show or demonstrate your expectations by modeling and guiding students through each step of a process. Provide clear guidelines and standards.

Bridging

Activate and build on students' prior knowledge. While students progress from the known to the unknown, help them make connections to previous learning. Use comprehensible input, and level questions to address levels of language proficiency.

Schema Building

Use graphic organizers to help students relate and connect old and new ideas. Start with a lesson's big ideas. Then guide students to add details.

Metacognitive Development

Encourage students to think about how they learn. Teach learning strategies and provide opportunities for practice. Use learning logs and reflective journals to help students evaluate their learning.

Text Representation

Involve students in representing information in another form. Encourage them to review what they know and to communicate this knowledge in new formats, such as illustrations, charts, diagrams, graphic organizers, symbols, and mathematical expressions.

Access Strategies and the Lesson Format

The goal of this book is to teach grade-level content and to develop English language proficiency. You can modify the strategies to meet the needs of students at various levels of language acquisition. Scaffolding structures are built into each lesson and a variety of language experiences are offered. Each lesson is organized in four parts as follows.

Motivation

This section includes ideas for starting the lesson. A variety of strategies address the different modalities of learning that are important for students learning English. Motivation involves all students, gains their attention and focus, and sets the tone for the lesson.

Concept Vocabulary

Successful lessons for ELLs include direct instruction of vocabulary. The lessons list possible vocabulary along with at least one activity to reinforce the words and concepts. The words should be used throughout the day and made part of students' working vocabulary. Repetition and reinforcement are essential. Activities may include extension of oral and/or written language, focusing on concept development.

Guided Instruction

Key concepts form the focal point for this section. Scaffolding structures and ideas for providing comprehensible input are available for each lesson. Strategies are typically interactive, and they accommodate different learning styles. Mixed-language groupings are often recommended to provide a student-centered, low-anxiety learning environment.

Integrating Language

This section provides strategies and ideas to reinforce content while you introduce and practice language structures with students. The incorporation of scaffolding structures ensures student success.

Sample Strategies and Best Practices

Oral Language

Role-Play

Invite students to imagine that they are characters or numbers in a problem. Then have them act out the solution.

Chant

To help students develop language, practice language skills, and learn language patterns, have them repeat words and phrases rhythmically.

Grand Conversation

Ask a group leader to record information as students join in a discussion of the text. Then have the leader report to the group on patterns in the responses.

Paraphrase

Have students retell ideas presented by the text, a teacher, or another student, using their own words.

Tableau

Students visualize and interpret an event that is shown in a photograph or illustration from the text. Students plan or study a scene. They develop a list of the various people in the scene and brainstorm the possible thoughts of each person. They assign roles and then place themselves in the scene and "freeze." A leader or the teacher taps a person in the scene who speaks "in character" while the others remain "frozen." An interview approach is an alternative.

Think Aloud Protocol

After you model, encourage students to work in pairs and take turns to think aloud their critical thinking skills.

Listing

Cued/Free Retell

Pairs of students use a prepared list of main ideas from the text to tape-record each other as they recall information. Checks are made on freely recalled information before students are cued to retell the remaining ideas.

Narrative Input Chart

On a chart in the style of flannel board stories, the teacher develops the mathematical concepts from the text. The visual representation of the concept may include drawings, copies of book pages, picture file cards, and manipulatives. The concept is explained using the visual representation. Then, students reiterate or expand upon the concept.

Reading

These techniques work well with word problems and with literature related to mathematics.

Choral Reading

A group oral reading form that works well across grade levels. The group reads a text together, reserving some parts for individuals or small groups.

Paired Reading

Students in pairs support each other as they each read the text aloud. A fluent reader supports a reader who may be having difficulty.

Pairs of students work together, usually reading a portion of a text. One student asks the other questions related to the content. The second student answers as many questions as possible. The roles are then reversed, with the second student asking questions and the first attempting to answer them. At strategic stopping points, students summarize what they have read.

Echo Reading

Students read in pairs. One student reads aloud as the other student follows and echoes the first reader. Support is provided to students who may have difficulty reading the text.

Written Language

Journal Entry

Students keep a journal that explains, in their own words, what they learned in class.

Double-Entry Journal

Students divide a sheet of paper into two columns. The first column is used to copy a word problem from the text. The second column is used to restate the problem in the student's own words.

Graphic Organizer

Students write on a class or individual graphic organizer. Ideas and concepts are recorded in appropriate places to organize thoughts and to structure content. Graphic organizers are often used later for planning, writing or speaking assignments.

Word Problems

Students write their own word problems using the concepts from a specific lesson.

Storyboard

Students illustrate steps of a word problem or model in sequence.

Cooperative Learning

Think-Pair-Share

The teacher poses a problem. Students determine a strategy that could be used to solve the problem and write the solution. Each student shares his or her ideas with a partner. Then the pair shares their solution with another pair or with the whole class.

Heads Together

The teacher poses a problem. Students work in pairs or in groups of four to collaborate and reach group consensus. One student in each group reports the response.

Numbered Heads Together

Groups of four students select a team name. Then each student in the group is assigned a number (1, 2, 3, 4). The teacher poses a question, and the students collaborate to make sure that everyone in the group is prepared to respond to the question. The teacher then chooses a team and a number at random. The student with that number responds to the question.

Jigsaw

Students in a group are each assigned to read a different part of the same selection. After reading, each student retells to the others in the group what he/she has read.

Bibliography

Archibald, J. (ed.) (2000). *Second Language Acquisition and Linguistic Theory.* Oxford: Blackwell.

Bilingual Education Handbook: Designing Instruction for LEP Students. (1990). Sacramento, CA; California Department of Education.

Campbell, L., Campbell, B., and Dickinson, D. (1999). *Teaching and Learning Through Multiple Intelligences.* Needham, MA: Allyn & Bacon.

Cantoni-Harvey, G. (1987). *Content-area language instruction: Approaches and strategies.* Reading, MA: Addison-Wesley.

Cummins, J. (1994). "The Acquisition of English as a Second Language" in *Kids Come in All Languages: Reading Instruction for ESL Students.* Newark, DE: International Reading Association.

Holt, Daniel (Ed.). (1993). *Cooperative learning: response to linguistic and cultural diversity.* Washington, D.C.: Center for Applied Linguistics.

Krashen, S. (1982). *Principles and practice in second language acquisition.* New York: Pergamon Press.

Krashen, S., and Terrell, T. (1983). *The natural approach.* San Francisco: Pergamon/Alemany Press.

Mohan, B. (1986). *Language and content.* Reading, MA: Addison-Wesley.

Randall, J.A. (Ed.). (1987). *ESL through content-area instruction.* Englewood Cliffs, NJ: Prentice Hall Regents/ERIC Clearinghouse on Languages and Linguistics. (ERIC Document Reproduction Service No. ED 283387)

Reyhner, J., and Davison, D.M. (1992). "Improving Mathematics and Science Instruction for LEP Middle and High School Students Through Language Activities" in *Third National Research Symposium on Limited English Proficient Student Issues.*

Schifini, Alfredo. (1991). "Language, Literacy, and Content Instruction: Strategies for Teachers" in *Kids Come in All Languages: Reading Instruction for ESL Students.* Newark, DE: International Reading Association.

Willetts, K. (Ed.). (1986). *Integrating language and content instruction.* Los Angeles: Center for Language Education and Research, UCLA. (ERIC Document Reproduction Service No. ED 278262)

Willetts, K., and Crandall, J.A. (1986). *Content-based language instruction.* ERIC/CLL News Bulletin, 9 (2). Washington, D.C.: ERIC Clearinghouse on Languages and Linguistics.

Place Value and Number Sense

KINESTHETIC ACTIVITY: Give each of five volunteers an index card on which is written a digit from 0 through 9. Have the volunteers stand in a line facing the class, holding their index cards so the class can see. Ask the class to record the number. Then have the volunteers rearrange themselves in a different order and have the class record the new number. Repeat the procedure several times. Then have a sixth volunteer, whose index card shows a comma, join the group. Have the class decide where the comma should be placed in the number currently being shown. Have the group rearrange themselves several times, each time deciding where the comma should be. Elicit that the placement of the comma remains the same, regardless of the numbers represented.

Materials: index cards; base-ten units, rods, and flats; Chapter 1 Worksheet

Concept Vocabulary: *period, thousands, millions*

Use base-ten blocks to demonstrate a 3-digit number. Have students identify the number. Write the number on the board.

Write the term *period* on the board and read it aloud. Ask students to give the common meaning of this word, and explain that in math it has a different meaning. Refer to the number on the board. Explain that each group of three digits is called a *period*.

Add to the base-ten block configuration created earlier in order to convert the number into a 4-digit number. Write the term *thousands* on the board and read it aloud. Lead students to understand that the new digit represents the *thousands* place value. Write the four-digit number on the chalkboard. Explain that a comma must be used to separate the periods. Add more blocks to create the *ten thousands* place value, revise the number written on the board, and explain the change. Repeat with the *hundred thousands* place value.

Write the term *millions* on the board. Use base-ten configurations as above to demonstrate the changes in value. Lead students to understand why a second comma must be added when the number is written in standard form. Challenge volunteers to write numbers with *ten millions* and *hundred millions* place values.

Guided Instruction

Create the following chart on the board. Guide students as they use the chart to apply their knowledge of the concept vocabulary. Make sure that students use commas to separate periods.

Write each number in standard form.	**Answer**
two thousand, four hundred thirty-nine	**(2,439)**
1 million + 10 thousands + 3 hundreds + 6 tens	**(1,010,360)**
8,000,000 + 100,000 + 1	**(8,100,001)**

Add further entries as needed to ensure comprehension. Then reverse the chart, guiding students as they use the vocabulary words to name numbers written in standard form.

Standard Form	**Word Form**
122,115	**(one hundred twenty-two thousand, one hundred fifteen)**
6,310,004	**(six million, three hundred ten thousand, four)**
12,050	**(twelve thousand, fifty)**

Add further entries as needed to ensure comprehension.

Have students take turns writing 4- to 7-digit numbers on the board. Have other students use the vocabulary words to identify the values of each digit.

Integrating Language

Have students use the Chapter 1 Worksheet to review and practice what they have learned. You might model the process by working with students to solve the first problem orally. After students have completed their independent work, measure comprehension by checking and discussing their answers.

Name ______________________

Place Value and Number Sense

Write the number in standard form. Be sure to separate each period with a comma.

1. two million, one thousand

   2,001,000

2. 3,000 + 400 + 6

   3,406

3. 8,000 + 400 + 90

   8,490

4. three million, four hundred thousand, nine hundred forty-five

   3,400,945

5. ten million, seven

   10,000,007

6. thirty-three thousand, four hundred five

   33,405

Use word form to write the value of the underlined digit.

7. 34,5<u>6</u>7,493 sixty thousand

8. <u>3</u>7,455,988 thirty million

9. 4,00<u>3</u>,987 three thousand

10. <u>5</u>47,675,009 five hundred million

11. <u>7</u>,939,067 seven million

12. How many periods are in each of the numbers in Exercises 7–11? 3

Compare and Order Whole Numbers

HANDS-ON EXPERIMENT: Display two pencils of different lengths and colors. Ask students to help you compare them, pointing out that comparing means telling how things are alike and different. Lead students to see that the items can be compared by color and by size, using such terms as *bigger than, smaller than, darker than, lighter than*, and so on. Then write two 3-digit numbers on the board. Remind students that they have learned to compare numbers.

Materials: chart paper, graph paper

Concept Vocabulary: *greater than, less than, round, nearest*

Write the first two vocabulary terms on the board and read them aloud. Point out that these terms can be used to compare numbers. If necessary, review the meanings of the terms and ask students to suggest synonyms for each. (bigger, larger; smaller, fewer) Use the two numbers you have written on the board as an example, using a sentence such as *Four hundred forty-two is greater than two hundred ninety-seven.* Then introduce the symbols $<$ and $>$. Use them to write comparisons of the numbers, such as $442 > 297$ and $297 < 442$. Repeat with a pair of 4-digit numbers.

Point out that the $<$ and $>$ symbols can be used to put a series of numbers in order, from either least to greatest or greatest to least. As an example, write the numbers 724, 798, and 767 on the chalkboard. Work with students to write the numbers from least to greatest, separating them with the appropriate symbol.

Write the terms *round* and *nearest* on the chalkboard and read them aloud. Use a variety of classroom objects to demonstrate that a particular object is *nearest* to you. Ask students to suggest different meanings for *round* that are already familiar to them. Point out that in math, this term can mean "to tell about how many." As an example, write the number 67 on the chalkboard. Tell students that you will *round* this number to the *nearest* ten, or 70. Have students take turns rounding other numbers to the nearest hundred, thousand, ten thousand, and so on.

Guided Instruction

Put the following chart on the board or on chart paper. Have students add either < or > to make true statements. Then have them read their completed entries aloud, using the vocabulary term *greater than* or *less than*.

Number	< or > ?	Number
5,467	(<)	5,647
3,450	(<)	34,300
57,009	(<)	75,001
4,896,298	(>)	489,973

Use a similar chart, such as the one below, to guide students as they use < and > marks to order series of numbers.

Number	Order	Answers
6,840 6,782 6,934	least to greatest	**(6,782 < 6,840 < 6,934)**
16,232 16,223 16,322	least to greatest	**(16,223 < 16,232 < 16,322)**
263,876 2,643,002 279,866	greatest to least	**(2,643,002 > 279,866 > 263,876)**
54,601,020 5,766,000 54,601,009	greatest to least	**(54,601,020 > 54,601,009 > 5,766,000)**

Use a chart similar to the following to guide students as they round numbers.

Number	Round to the nearest. . . .	Answer
343	hundred	**(300)**
1,879	thousand	**(2,000)**
121,988	hundred thousand	**(100,000)**
3,624,387	ten thousand	**(3,620,000)**

Integrating Language

Have students work with partners to make similar charts to challenge other sets of partners. Encourage them to use the classroom charts as models. Provide time for partners to complete their charts and to present orally to the group one or more completed entries. Have them use the vocabulary terms in their presentations. Check all written work for accuracy.

Add and Subtract Whole Numbers

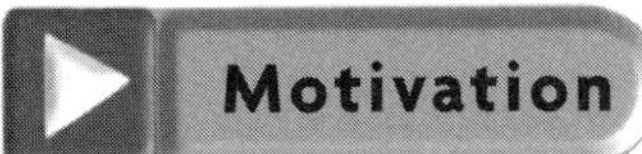

DEMONSTRATION: Draw two arrows on the chalkboard, one facing to the left and the other facing to the right. Give volunteers simple directions to follow, pointing to the arrows in place of the words for *left* and *right*. Examples might include, *Take 2 steps to the →. Move 3 steps to the ←.* After several demonstrations, ask students to explain how the volunteers knew which way to move. (**the arrow symbols**) Then explain that a math problem also contains a sign that gives directions for finding the answer. Write + and − on the board and discuss the operation indicated by each sign. As examples, write $7 + 5 =$ and $7 - 5 =$. Guide students to use the signs to solve the problems.

Materials: Chapter 3 Worksheet

Concept Vocabulary: *sum, difference, exact, estimate*

Write the terms *sum* and *difference* on the chalkboard and read them aloud. Refer to the math problems above. Explain that the answer to an addition problem is called the *sum* and the answer to a subtraction problem is called the *difference*. Write several simple addition and subtraction problems on the board. Have students use the operation signs to decide whether each problem requires that they find a sum or a difference. If time allows, have them solve the problems.

Write the terms *exact* and *estimate* on the board and read them aloud. Ask a volunteer to find the sum of 8 + 19. Point out that 27 is the *exact* answer.

Remind students that they have learned how to *round* numbers. If necessary, review the process. Then explain that often, finding the exact answer is easier if you first *estimate* it—or tell about how many—by rounding. Use as an example 8 + 19. First, point out that 8 can be rounded to 10, and 19 can be rounded to 20. Therefore, an estimate of the answer is $10 + 20 = 30$. Then remind students that they found the exact answer earlier. Stress how close 27 is to the estimate. Explain that estimating the answer to an addition or subtraction problem can help them to decide whether their exact answer is reasonable.

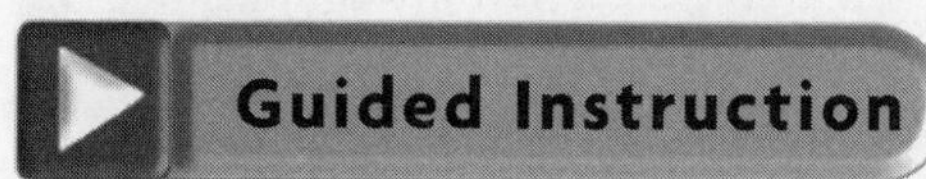

Guided Instruction

On the board, write a series of addition and subtraction problems such as:

$$\begin{array}{r} 623 \\ +\ 13 \\ \hline \end{array} \qquad \begin{array}{r} 822 \\ -423 \\ \hline \end{array} \qquad \begin{array}{r} 613 \\ +149 \\ \hline \end{array}$$

Provide at least one problem for each student. Then have students take turns using the operation sign to decide what the problem requires, and then state the directions in a sentence containing a vocabulary term (*Find the sum; Find the difference*). Then have the student solve the problem. Point out that when they read the directions for solving problems in their textbooks or on tests, they should look carefully for the word *sum* or *difference*. Then they should double-check their understanding of what to do by looking at the operation sign in each problem.

Erase the answers to all problems on the board. Review the concept of *greatest place value*. Then work with students to estimate the sums and differences by rounding the numbers to the greatest place value. Ask students to tell why estimating is a valuable first step in finding sums and differences. Point out that they should read the directions for solving problems in their textbooks or on tests carefully. If the directions ask *How many?*, they should find the *exact* answer. If, on the other hand, the directions ask *About how many?*, they should find an *estimate*.

Integrating Language

Have students use the Chapter 3 Worksheet to review the vocabulary terms and practice following the specifics of written directions. You might model the process by working with students to solve the first problem orally. After students have completed their independent work, measure comprehension by checking and discussing their answers.

Name ______________________________

Add and Subtract Whole Numbers

Find the sum or difference.

1. $\begin{array}{r} 459 \\ +\ 342 \\ \hline 801 \end{array}$

2. $\begin{array}{r} 6{,}005 \\ +\ 987 \\ \hline 6{,}992 \end{array}$

3. $\begin{array}{r} 5{,}906 \\ -\ 1{,}372 \\ \hline 4{,}534 \end{array}$

4. $\begin{array}{r} 98{,}519 \\ -\ 33{,}620 \\ \hline 64{,}899 \end{array}$

5. $\begin{array}{r} \$4.09 \\ -\ \$3.72 \\ \hline \$0.37 \end{array}$

6. $\begin{array}{r} \$2.99 \\ +\ \$1.07 \\ \hline \$4.06 \end{array}$

Find the sum. Estimate to check.

7. $\begin{array}{r} 203 \\ +\ 39 \\ \hline 242 \end{array}$

8. $\begin{array}{r} 5{,}097 \\ +\ 780 \\ \hline 5{,}877 \end{array}$

9. $\begin{array}{r} 7{,}821 \\ +\ 1{,}463 \\ \hline 9{,}284 \end{array}$

10. $\begin{array}{r} 28{,}282 \\ +\ 53{,}009 \\ \hline 81{,}291 \end{array}$

11. $\begin{array}{r} \$24.54 \\ +\ \$67.72 \\ \hline \$92.26 \end{array}$

12. $\begin{array}{r} \$8{,}420 \\ +\ \$3{,}712 \\ \hline \$12{,}132 \end{array}$

13. $\begin{array}{r} \$1{,}098 \\ +\ \$1{,}881 \\ \hline \$2{,}979 \end{array}$

14. $\begin{array}{r} 32{,}518 \\ +\ 27{,}463 \\ \hline 59{,}981 \end{array}$

15. $\begin{array}{r} 205{,}009 \\ +\ 142{,}315 \\ \hline 347{,}324 \end{array}$

Find the difference. Estimate to check.

16. 392 − 19

373

17. 4,223 − 877

3,346

18. 3,701 − 2,709

992

19. 52,997 − 9

52,988

20. \$8.97 − \$1.04

\$7.93

21. 6,428 − 3,119

3,309

22. 9,998 − 1,023

8,975

23. 44,518 − 22,372

22,146

24. 90,005 − 23,187

66,818

25. At the stamp collectors' fair, Ari bought 8 stamps from Kenya, 17 stamps from Mexico, and 11 stamps from Japan. About how many stamps did he buy?

about 40 stamps

26. In her garden, Aunt Maria planted 14 tulip bulbs and 27 daffodil bulbs. How many bulbs did she plant in all?

41 bulbs

Chapter 4

Algebra: Use Addition and Subtraction

Motivation

DISCUSSION: On the board, write the following expressions:

12 + 9   12 − 9

Elicit from students the meaning of each operation sign and what they would be asked to find (**sum, difference**) in each problem. Have volunteers come to the board to write the sum and the difference. If necessary, point out that to be complete, each problem needs an equal sign.

12 + 9 = 21   12 − 9 = 3

Repeat the procedure with several other examples, each time having students include an equal sign when they write a sum or a difference.

Materials: chart paper, markers

Concept Vocabulary: *expression, equation, parentheses, variable*

Write the terms *equation* and *expression* on the board and read them aloud. Refer to the completed equations from the Motivation activity. Point out that *equation* is another term for number sentence. Have students take turns writing sample addition and subtraction equations on the board. Then cover the equal sign and answer on one of the equations. Explain that an *expression* is a part of an equation. It contains numbers and operations signs, but it does not contain an equal sign.

Write the following expressions on the board:

(2 + 8) − 3   6 + (9 − 4)   15 − (2 + 1 + 6)

Point out that each of these expressions contains two or more operation signs. Then write the term *parentheses* on the board and read it aloud. Ask a volunteer to identify the parentheses in each expression. Explain that operations within the parentheses should be done first. Model the process by showing the steps to take to find the value of the first expression. Then have students help you find the value of the remaining expressions.

Write the following equations on the board:

2 + □ = 7   6 − □ = 5

Review with students the process to use to find the missing numbers in an addition or subtraction problem. Then rewrite the equations, using a lowercase letter in place of the box. Write the term *variable* on the board and read it aloud. Point out that like a box, a *variable* is a letter or symbol that stands for a missing number.

$2 + x = 7$ $\quad\quad$ $6 - y = 5$

Remind students that they have learned how to find missing numbers in problems. Work with them to find the value of each variable.

Guided Instruction

On chart paper, write a series of simple addition and subtraction expressions, such as 18 + 29, 43 − 24, and so on. Write at least one expression for each student. Ask students to tell whether they are expressions or equations. Then have students take turns changing each expression into an equation and solving it.

Repeat with a series of simple expressions containing parentheses, such as 12 + (13 − 2), (24 + 7) − 14, 72 − (20 + 13 + 3), and so on. Write at least one expression for each student. Ask students to tell whether they are expressions or equations. Ask them what the curved marks are called, and what they mean. Then have students take turns changing each expression into an equation and solving it.

Repeat with a series of simple equations containing variables, such as $24 + x = 31$, $82 - b = 17$, $45 + k = 56$, and so on. Write at least one equation for each student. Ask students to tell whether they are expressions or equations. Ask them what the letters are called. Then have students take turns solving each equation.

Integrating Language

Have students use each of the letters in their first names as variables as they write a series of expressions. Have them trade papers with partners. Direct each partner to turn the expressions into equations and solve them. Close by having students use the vocabulary words to describe their thinking with sentences such as the following:

I have the expression 17 + (4 − 3).
I can use a variable to show the unknown value: $17 + (4 - 3) = t$.
I know that I should find the value of the expression in parentheses first.
4 − 3 = 1.
17 + 1 = 18 is my equation.

Chapter 5

Understand Time

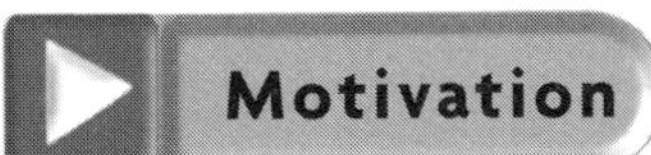

Motivation

KINESTHETIC ACTIVITY: Have students work with partners to time themselves completing a number of tasks, such as writing their names 10 times, writing the letters of the alphabet backward, or finding a word in a dictionary. (Students may use stopwatches for this activity, or a clock with a second hand.) You may wish to model the process before students begin. Have partners share their results.

Materials: stopwatch, calendar page, Chapter 5 Worksheet

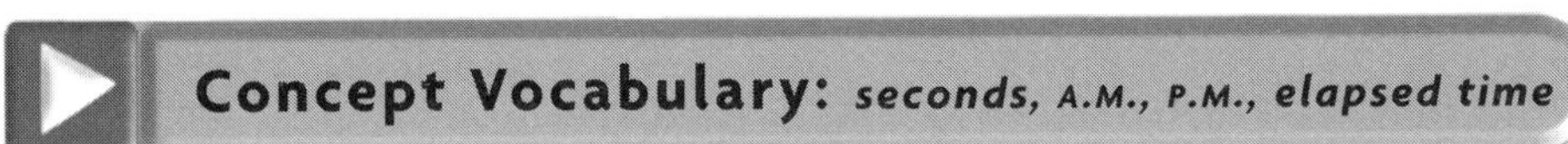

Concept Vocabulary: ***seconds, A.M., P.M., elapsed time***

Write the term *seconds* on the board and read it aloud. Be sure students understand that in this lesson, *second* refers to a measure of time rather than the order of a series of events (first, second, third). Explain that just as every hour is divided into 60 minutes, each minute is divided into 60 seconds. Point out the second hand on the classroom clock or on a wristwatch.

Then write A.M. and P.M. on the board and read them aloud. Point out that these terms are abbreviations that stand for the hours between midnight and noon and the hours between noon and midnight. (You may wish to explain to students who are more familiar with a 24-hour clock, that A.M. is used for the hours 1–12 while P.M. is used for the hours 13–24.) Give such examples as, *I eat breakfast at about 7:15 A.M. When do you eat breakfast?* and *On school nights, I usually go to bed around 9:30 P.M. When do you usually go to bed on school nights?* Ask additional questions to provide each student with at least one opportunity to respond. Remind students to use the terms A.M. and P.M. in their responses.

Write the term *elapsed time* on the board and read it aloud. Explain that it means the amount of time that passes from the start of an activity to the end of that activity. Tell students that when they timed each other completing a task for the Motivation activity, they were recording the elapsed time. Draw a clockface on the board to show students how they can use a clock to find the elapsed time in examples such as the following.

start: 8:45 A.M.
end: 11:30 A.M.

start: 6:00 P.M.
end: 9:15 P.M.

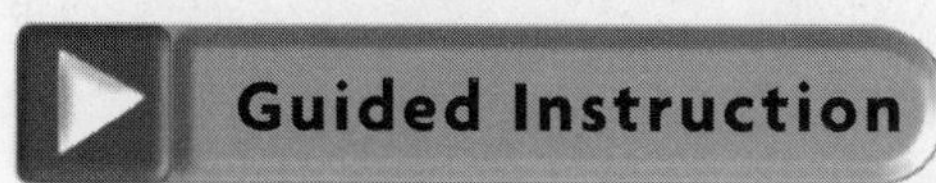

Guided Instruction

Draw an analog clockface and a digital clockface on the board. Lead students to express various times in words, including *seconds*. Use such examples as 6:10, 5 seconds; 9:30, 15 seconds; and so on.

Put the schedule below on the board. Work with students to compute the amount of elapsed time during each event. Then ask such questions as, *Did Game Time! take place in the morning or the afternoon? How did you know?* (**A.M. designation**); *Which two events or classes took the same amount of elapsed time?* (**Morning Meeting and Share Ideas**); and *How many minutes elapsed between Game Time! and Lunch?* (**10 minutes**)

Computer Camp Schedule

Activity	Time	Elapsed Time
Morning Meeting	9:00 A.M.–9:40 A.M.	**(40 minutes)**
Programmers' Class	9:45 A.M.–10:35 A.M.	**(50 minutes)**
Game Time!	10:45 A.M.–11:50 A.M.	**(1 hour, 5 minutes)**
Lunch	noon–1:10 P.M.	**(1 hour, 10 minutes)**
Internet Instruction	1:15 P.M.–2:30 P.M.	**(1 hour, 15 minutes)**
Meet an Expert	2:30 P.M.–3:05 P.M.	**(35 minutes)**
Share Ideas	3:15 P.M.–3:55 P.M.	**(40 minutes)**

Display a blank calendar page. If necessary, review the English names for the days of the week and the months of the year. Then fill in appointments on the calendar page, such as "piano lesson, 2:30 P.M." Work with students to use the calendar to tell how many hours, days, or weeks elapse between various appointments and events.

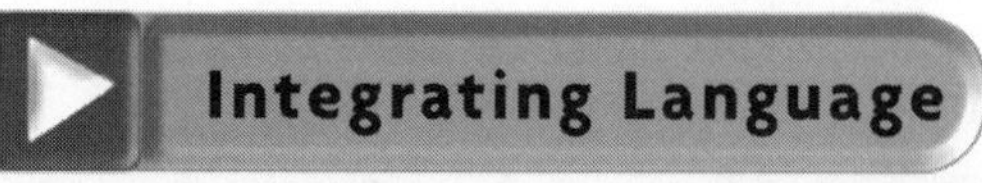

Integrating Language

Have students use the Chapter 5 Worksheet to review and practice what they have learned. You might model the process by working with students to solve the first problem orally. After students have completed their independent work, measure comprehension by checking and discussing their answers.

Name ______________________________

Understand Time

Draw lines to connect the clock or watch with the correct time.

1. 

2. 

3. 

4. 

5. 

6. 

a. fifteen minutes before seven

b. twenty-seven seconds

c. 15 minutes, 27 seconds after 6

d. midnight

e. three thirty

f. seven minutes and forty-five seconds after three

Complete the schedule to show elapsed time.

Play Rehearsal Schedule

	Activity	Time	Elapsed Time
7.	Staff Meeting	9:00 A.M.–9:45 A.M.	45 minutes
8.	Set Building	9:50 A.M.–10:45 A.M.	55 minutes
9.	Actors' Rehearsal	10:55 A.M.–noon	1 hr., 5 min.
10.	Dancers' Rehearsal	noon–2:25 P.M.	2 hrs., 25 min.

Use the calendar to answer the questions.

August

Sunday	Monday	Tuesday	Wednesday	Thursday	Friday	Saturday
		1	2	3	4	5
6	7	8	9	10	11	12
13	14	15	16	17	18	19
20	21	22	23	24	25	26
27	28	29	30	31		

11. The Stamp Club meets on the first and third Friday of every month. On what dates will they meet in August?

August 4 and 18

12. On the Monday before her birthday, Jen received a package in the mail. Her birthday is August 17. On what date did she receive the package?

August 14

Chapter 6

Collect and Organize Data

DEMONSTRATION: Tell students that you are going to take a survey to collect data about their favorite types of pets. Have each student name his or her favorite type of pet and list responses on the board. Point out responses that repeat, eliciting that in order to be useful the survey information has to be organized in some way. Ask students to brainstorm ways the information could be organized. If time allows, try out some of their ideas.

Materials: chart paper, books from classroom library

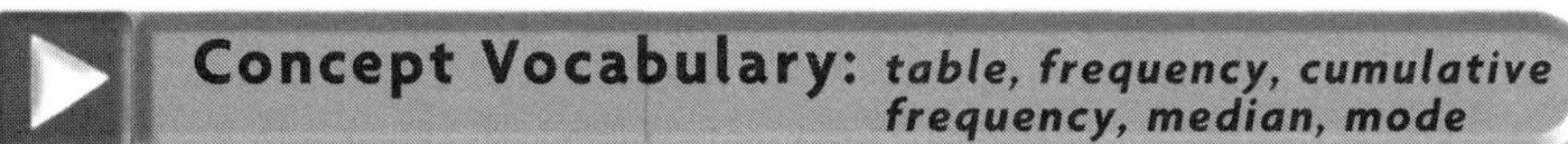

Write *table* on the board and read it aloud. Have students tell the common meaning of this word, and then lead them to understand its meaning as a mathematical term ("a form that helps to organize data"). Then write *frequency table* and *cumulative frequency* on the board and read them aloud. Point out that *frequency* means "how often." Therefore, a *frequency table* is a form that helps you organize data based on how often each survey result occurs. On the board or on chart paper, create a frequency table similar to the one below to organize data regarding students' favorite pets, asking questions such as *How often was the response "dog" given? How often was the response "cat" given?*

Pet	Frequency	Cumulative Frequency

Explain that the *cumulative frequency* column is used to keep track of the number of people surveyed.

Write the words *median* and *mode* on the board and read them aloud. Explain that once data is collected and organized, it can be analyzed. Tell students that the *mode* is the value that occurs most often in the data, and identify the mode in the pet survey. Then tell students that when the data is organized from least to greatest, the *median* is the number in the middle.

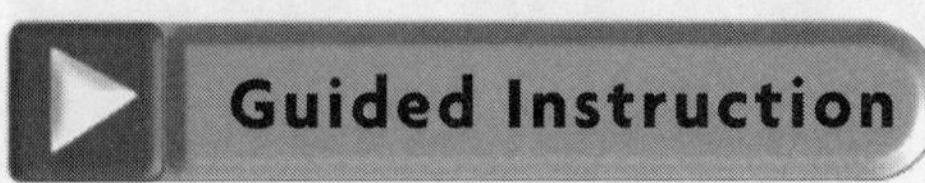

Have students gather data or present them with information such as the ticket data shown below. Work with them to create a tally sheet and then a frequency table to record their results. When the table is complete, have students use the words *table, frequency,* and *cumulative frequency* to describe how they organized the data.

Concert Tickets Sold	
Day	**Tickets**
Monday	15
Tuesday	28
Wednesday	12
Thursday	28
Friday	16

Next, help students find the median (**16**) and the mode (**28**). To make finding the median and the mode easier, you might work with students to sort the numbers from least to greatest value. Point out that often there may be more than one mode, or there may be no mode at all.

Integrating Language

Have students work in small groups. Assign specific sets of data for them to use to create frequency tables and to find the medians and the modes. You might have them survey group members regarding favorite games, songs, birds, flowers, and so on. Allow time for groups to present their tables to the class, using the vocabulary words to summarize how they organized their data.

Analyze and Graph Data

CREATE ILLUSTRATIONS: Challenge students to work with a partner to create pictures that show your local weather for the last week. Tell partners to begin by recalling temperatures, precipitation, and other weather conditions. Next tell students to plan their pictures. Will they show seven different images on one sheet of paper? Will they use different sheets of paper to draw the image for each day? How will they indicate which picture represents a particular day? How will they show how warm or cold it was? Display several examples of the finished products.

Materials: chart paper, Chapter 7 Worksheet

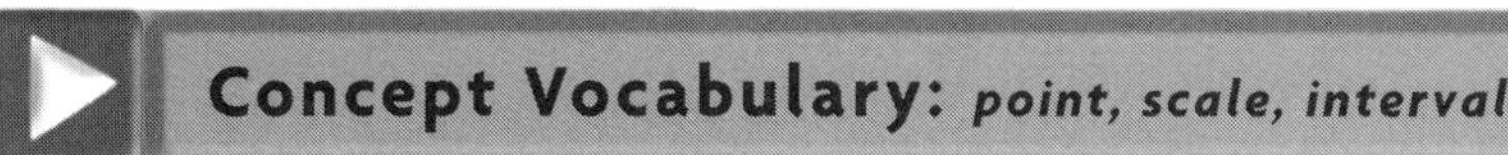

Tell students that their pictures from the Motivation activity represent one way to show how something changes over a period of time. Explain that in this lesson they will be looking at another way to show such change. On chart paper, make the following line graph.

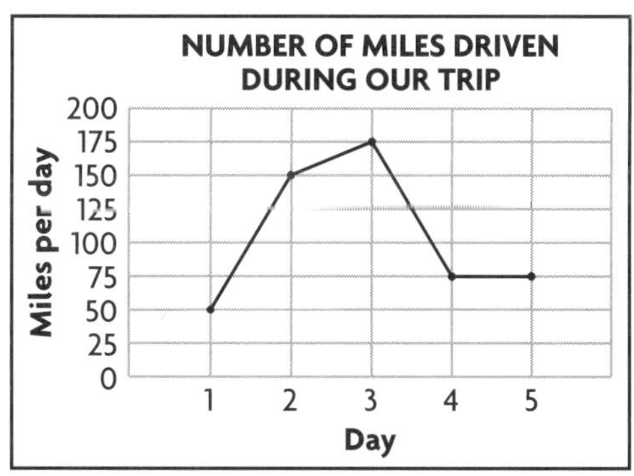

Elicit from students that this is a line graph. Ask students to tell what the title of the line graph is. Point out that a student made this line graph to plot the number of miles that he and his family drove each day during a 5-day trip. Point out how each day is represented on the line graph.

Write the term *point* on the board and read it aloud. Some students may be familiar with the use of *point* to describe a gesture. Explain that *point* has a mathematical meaning as well. Lead students to understand that each *point* on the graph marks the number of miles driven in a day. Have students take turns coming to the chart to identify each daily point.

Then write the terms *scale* and *interval* on the board and read them aloud. Lead students to understand that the *scale* of a graph shows the range of the data. Point out the scale of this graph. Then lead students to understand that the range is broken down into equal steps, or *intervals*. Point out that the interval of this graph is 25. Show students how the interval markings increase as 0, 25, 50, 75, and so on. Then work with students to use the scale, interval, and points to answer such questions as: *How many miles did they drive on Day 2? On what day did they drive the fewest miles? the most miles? How many more miles did they drive on Day 2 than they did on Day 1? How many miles did they drive in all?*

Guided Instruction

Work with students to convert the data on the following table into a line graph on chart paper or the board. You might add further games in order to give each student a turn to plot a point. Use a scale of 30 and an interval of 5. Have students take turns writing the title, labels, and scale numbers; plotting the points; and connecting the points with lines. Guide them as to the placement of such points as 18 and 7.

Jim's Basketball Team	
Game	**Baskets**
Game 1	15
Game 2	20
Game 3	10
Game 4	18
Game 5	7

Have students use the completed line graph to answer questions similar to those asked for the Miles Driven graph.

Have students work independently or with partners to use the Chapter 7 Worksheet to review and practice what they have learned. Measure comprehension by checking and discussing their completed graphs; by having them identify the scale, interval, and each specific point; and by answering questions that require them to use and compare data.

Analyze and Graph Data

The fourth graders sold tickets to the school band concert. The table shows how many tickets were sold each day.

Follow these steps to make a line graph of the data. Use the grid below.

Check students' graphs.

Concert Tickets Sold	
Day	**Number of Tickets**
Monday	2
Tuesday	10
Wednesday	7
Thursday	4
Friday	8

1. Write a title.
2. Use a scale of 0 to 12 and an interval of 2. Write the scale numbers along the left side of the graph.
3. Use the days as labels across the bottom of the graph.
4. Plot each point. Connect the points with a line.

____

Chapter 8

Practice Multiplication and Division Facts

DISCUSSION: On the chalkboard draw five boxes and shade the first two boxes. Have a student write two addition equations for the boxes. **($2 + 3 = 5$; $3 + 2 = 5$)** Discuss the Commutative Property of Addition. Make sure they remember that it does not matter in what order the addends are added.

Ask, *What is the opposite of addition?* **(subtraction)**
Have another student write two subtraction equations for the boxes. **($5 - 2 = 3$; $5 - 3 = 2$)**

Discuss why the Commutative Property does not apply to subtraction. **($5 - 3$ and $3 - 5$ do not have the same answer; $5 - 2$ and $2 - 5$ do not have the same answer.)**

Ask what name is given to the 4 equations they wrote. **(fact family)**

Concept Vocabulary: ***inverse operation, fact family, Zero Property, Identity Property, Commutative Property, Associative Property***

On the chalkboard write *fact family* and have a student define it. **(a set of equations using the same numbers)**

Write *inverse operation*. Explain that an inverse operation undoes another operation. *What is the inverse operation of subtraction?* **(addition)** *What other operation is an inverse operation?* **(Multiplication is the opposite of division; it is the inverse operation of division; multiplication undoes division.)**

On the board draw a 3 by 5 array and have students take turns writing the fact family.
($3 \times 5 = 15$; $5 \times 3 = 15$; $15 \div 3 = 5$; $15 \div 5 = 3$)

Write *Commutative Property*. Lead students to realize that this property applies to multiplication but not division. 3×5 and 5×3 have the same answer; $15 \div 3$ and $3 \div 15$ do not have the same answer.

Write *Associative Property*. Write $3 + 4 + 5$. Have students show 2 different ways to group the numbers.

$(3 + (4 + 5) = 12; (3 + 4) + 5 = 12)$
Elicit that because the sums the same, we can use this property with addition.

Write $2 \times 3 \times 4$ and have students write 2 different ways to show the Associative Property of Multiplication.
$(2 \times (3 \times 4) = 12; (2 \times 3) \times 4 = 12)$

Guided Instruction

On the board write the headings of the chart below.
Work with the students to organize what they have learned in the chart. Have them name the pairs of inverse operations. Have them give examples such as those shown below to illustrate the other properties.

Inverse Operations	Fact Family	Zero Property	Identity Property	Commutative Property	Associative Property
Addition	$3 + 6 = 9$ $6 + 3 = 9$	$5 + 0 = 5$ $0 + 5 = 5$	$5 + 0 = 5$ $0 + 5 = 5$	$4 + 3 = 7$ $3 + 4 = 7$	$4 + (3 + 2) = 9$ $(4 + 3) + 2 = 9$
Subtraction	$9 - 3 = 6$ $9 - 6 = 3$	$5 - 0 = 5$ $5 - 5 = 0$	$5 - 0 = 5$ $5 - 5 = 0$	no	no
Multiplication	$3 \times 6 = 18$ $6 \times 3 = 18$	$9 \times 0 = 0$ $0 \times 9 = 0$	$8 \times 1 = 8$ $1 \times 8 = 8$	$4 \times 3 = 12$ $3 \times 4 = 12$	$(1 \times 2) \times 3 = 6$ $1 \times (2 \times 3) = 6$
Division	$18 \div 6 = 3$ $18 \div 3 = 6$	$0 \div 9 = 0$ no	$8 \div 1 = 8$ $8 \div 8 = 1$	no	no

Integrating Language

Have a student tell how the Zero Property of Multiplication is different from the Zero Property of Addition. **(The product of zero and any number is zero, but the sum of any number and zero is that number.)**

Have a student explain why there are only 3 equations for the fact family of 0, 9, 0. **(We do not divide by zero.)**

State the Identity Property of Multiplication: *The product of 1 and any number is that number.* The Identity Property of Addition: *The sum of 0 and any number is that number.* Explain that Zero Property and Identity Property of Addition are the same. **$(1 + 0 = 1)$**, but those properties for multiplication are different. **$(1 \times 6 = 6, 0 \times 6 = 0)$**

Write this puzzle on the board.

$B \times B = G$	$M \times G = M$	$D \times B = B$
$2 \times 2 = 4$	$0 \times 4 = 0$	$1 \times 2 = 2$

Tell students the letters M, D, B, and G stand for the numbers 0, 1, 2, and 4 but not in the same order. Have them try to write the equations using the correct numbers.

Chapter 9

Algebra: Use Multiplication and Division Facts

DEMONSTRATION: Have students work in pairs for the following activity. Provide each pair with a list of words such as those shown below.

- baseball, golf ball, basketball, marble
- bird, horse, dog, cat
- pen, pencil, crayon, marker
- boot, sneaker, shoe, sandal

Ask the partners to decide on a method to put the listed items in sequence. Have pairs present their sequenced lists to the class and have the class identify the method used to determine the sequence. (**Possible answers for the method used to sequence the lists include alphabetical order, smallest to largest, or lightest to heaviest. Accept reasonable answers.**)

Materials: chart paper, Chapter 9 Worksheet

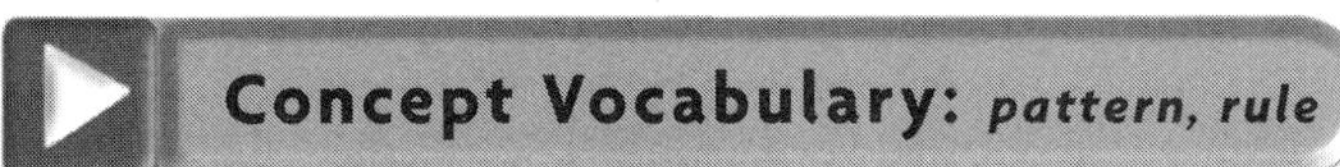

Write these expressions on the board.

$(8 \div 2) + 7$ $(3 \times 2) + 8$ $(4 \times 3) + (10 \div 5)$

Explain the function of parentheses, stressing that to find the values of such expressions, students should:

1. do the operation inside the parentheses,

2. do any other operations within the expression.

Write the terms *pattern* and *rule* on the board and read them aloud. Some students may be familiar with more commonly used meanings for these terms. Tell students they can use what they know about the meanings of these terms to better understand their mathematical meanings. Then write the following pattern on the board:

3, 8, 13, 18

Remind students that in the Motivation activity, they chose a method to put items in a sequence. Point out that the rest of the class had to look for a *pattern* to figure out the method used. Explain that the intervals between the numbers form a *pattern*; each interval is equal in value. Use loops to count and mark the numbers between 3 and 8, 8 and 13, and so on. Ask students what the next number in the pattern would be. (**23**) Then point out that this pattern follows a *rule*. The rule is "Add 5." Explain that in math, a *rule* means "something that is always true." Write other number patterns on the board and ask students to find the rules.

Guided Instruction

On the board, write a series of expressions containing parentheses. Have students work with partners. Have each set of partners take turns coming to the board. At the board, have one partner give directions about the order of operations, while the other partner follows the directions to find the value of the expression. Monitor all directions and operations for accuracy. Repeat until each student has had the opportunity to serve as both director and solver.

Input	Output
x	y
2	6
4	8
6	10

On the board or on chart paper, reproduce the input/output table at the left.

Work with students to find a pattern between each input and output entry. Elicit from them that the rule is "Add 4." Use the variables to write the rule as the equation $x + 4 = y$. Stress that to be sure the rule is correct, you must test the rule on each pair of numbers in the table. Have students use the terms *pattern* and *rule* to explain what number would appear in the output column if the number 10 were added to the input column.

Integrating Language

Have students use the Chapter 9 Worksheet to review and practice what they have learned. Measure comprehension by checking and discussing their answers.

Algebra: Use Multiplication and Division Facts

Find the value of each variable.

1. $(16 \div 2) - 7 = n$

$n = 1$

2. $(2 \times 3) - 1 = k$

$k = 5$

3. $(5 \times 7) + 9 = t$

$t = 44$

4. $(36 \div 9) + 8 = e$

$e = 12$

5. $(9 \div 3) + (2 \times 1) = y$

$y = 5$

6. $(7 \times 3) - (2 \times 6) = w$

$w = 9$

7. $(54 \div 6) + (3 \times 6) = q$

$q = 27$

8. $(63 \div 7) + (18 \div 6) = y$

$y = 12$

9. $(27 \div 3) - (16 \div 2) = q$

$q = 1$

10. $(2 \times 3) \times (6 \div 2) = m$

$m = 18$

Look for a pattern. Find the rule. Write the rule in words. Then write it as an equation.

11.

Input	Output
g	*b*
6	36
8	48
10	60

Rule in words: multiply by 6

Equation: $g \times 6 = b$

12.

Input	Output
a	*c*
24	12
10	5
8	4

Rule in words: divide by 2

Equation: $a \div 2 = c$

Chapter 10

Multiply by 1-Digit Numbers

Motivation

HANDS-ON DEMONSTRATION: Read aloud: *Maria bought three boxes of notecards. Each box contained twelve cards. How many notecards did Maria buy?* Have volunteers use base-ten blocks to build models of three groups of twelve. Lead them to state the expression as 3 × 12. Remind them that to solve this problem in their heads, they might round 12 to the nearest ten, and calculate (3 × 10) + (3 × 2).

Materials: base-ten blocks

Concept Vocabulary: *group, regroup*

Write the terms *group* and *regroup* on the board and read them aloud. Refer to the model made with base-ten blocks above. Use it to explain the term *group*. Then draw attention to *regroup*. Explain that the word part *re-* often means "again." Therefore, the term *regroup* means "to group again," or "to make new groups."

Use base-ten blocks to demonstrate how to regroup. Remind students of the problem in the Motivation activity. Explain that when they rounded 12 to the nearest ten to calculate (3 × 10) + (3 × 2), they regrouped. Show students how to build a model to show the new expression.

Guided Instruction

Write the expression 3 × 127 on the board. Point out that when we multiply large numbers, we can start by grouping and regrouping.

Use base-ten blocks to make 3 groups of 127. Identify them as *groups*. Then model how to combine the ones (3 × 7 ones = 21 ones). Explain that you will now *regroup* 21 ones as 2 tens 1 one. Change the model accordingly. Then model how to combine the tens (3 × 2 tens = 6 tens). Add in the regrouped tens (6 tens + 2 regrouped tens = 8 tens). Change the model accordingly. Finally, model how to combine the hundreds (3 × 1 hundred = 3 hundreds).

Work with students to write the product in expanded form (**3 hundreds, 8 tens, 1 one**). Then write the product in standard form, as 381.

Repeat with additional expressions, asking students to direct you as you *group* and *regroup* to find the value of various multiplication expressions. Use expressions that call for regrouping of only the ones, only the tens, and both the ones and the tens. Allow each student at least one turn as "director."

Integrating Language

Write 5 to 10 word problems such as the following. Read them aloud to the students, write them on the board, or photocopy and distribute them on individual worksheets. Have students work with partners or independently to solve the word problems.

1. Julio and his father deliver the daily newspaper to 136 homes. How many papers do they deliver in 5 days? (**680 papers**)
2. Anna bought 8 boxes of paper clips. Each box cost $1.99. How much did Anna spend in all? (**$15.92**)

Allow time for students to explain the solving strategies they used, incorporating the terms *group* and *regroup* into their explanations.

Chapter 11

Multiply by Tens

Motivation

HANDS-ON ACTIVITY: Hold the 12 pencils in one hand and say, *I will* distribute *these pencils to 2 students.* Give one student 10 pencils and the other 2 pencils. On the chalkboard write $12 = 10 + 2$.

Have a student take all the pencils and show another way to *distribute* the pencils into two groups and write the number sentence, for example, $12 = 5 + 7$.

Have another student take all the pencils and show a way to *distribute* the pencils into three groups and write the number sentence, for example, $12 = 4 + 2 + 6$.

Ask, *In each of these sentences what is the number 12 called?* **(sum)** *What are the other numbers called?* **(addends)**

Materials: 12 pencils

Concept Vocabulary: ***The Distributive Property***

On the board, write *The Distributive Property*. Explain that the *Distributive Property* states that multiplying a sum by a number is the same as multiplying each addend by the number and then adding the products.

Write $12 = 10 + 2$. Ask, *What is the sum?* **(12)** *What are the addends?* **(10 and 2)**
Say, *The Distributive Property states that if I multiply 12 by 3, I will get the same answer as if I multiply 10 by 3 and 2 by 3 and add those answers.* Work together to solve.

$$\begin{array}{rrcrrcrr} & 12 & = & & 10 & + & & 2 \\ \times & 3 & & \times & 3 & & \times & 3 \\ \hline & 36 & = & & 30 & + & & 6 \end{array}$$

Say, *Did we get the same answer?* **(yes, $3 \times 12 = 36$ and $36 = 30 + 6$)**

Guided Instruction

Work with the students to solve the other problems they wrote earlier. Have them state the Distributive Property as they solve each part.

$$\begin{array}{rcrcr} 12 & = & 5 & + & 7 \\ \times\ 3 & & \times\ 3 & & \times\ 3 \\ \hline 36 & = & 15 & + & 21 \end{array}$$

and

$$\begin{array}{rcrcrcr} 12 & = & 4 & + & 2 & + & 6 \\ \times\ 3 & & \times\ 3 & & \times\ 3 & & \times\ 3 \\ \hline 36 & = & 12 & + & 6 & + & 18 \end{array}$$

Have students discuss which problem was easiest to solve. Lead them to understand that in this instance it may be easier just to multiply 12 by 3 than to use the Distributive Property. But for greater numbers the Distributive Property may make the problem simpler.

Write 8 × 49. Have students solve this using expanded form.

$$\begin{array}{rcrcrcr} 49 & = & 40 & + & 9 & & \\ \times\ 8 & & \times\ 8 & & \times\ 8 & & \\ \hline & & 320 & + & 72 & = & 392 \end{array}$$

Integrating Language

Write these problems on the board for students to solve on their own papers. Then discuss the problems to see which students used the Distributive Property and why.

9 × 85   7 × 68   5 × 79   6 × 57

Multiply by 2-Digit Numbers

HANDS-ON REVIEW: Challenge students to solve the following multiplication problems as quickly as they can. Encourage students to use basic facts as well as other strategies they have learned. **(432; 18,630; 62,730)**

$$\begin{array}{r} 27 \\ \times 16 \\ \hline \end{array} \qquad \begin{array}{r} 345 \\ \times\ 54 \\ \hline \end{array} \qquad \begin{array}{r} 1,845 \\ \times\ \ \ 34 \\ \hline \end{array}$$

Use the problems to review the terms *partial products* and *simpler problems* and the use of rounding and estimating to decide whether an exact answer is reasonable. You may also wish to reinforce the idea that they should follow the same steps to multiply greater numbers that they follow to multiply lesser numbers.

Materials: Chapter 12 Worksheet

Concept Vocabulary: *decimal point, multistep, multistep problem*

Write these numbers on the board for students to read. Have them write and read the numbers using a dollar sign and decimal point.

5¢	35¢	426¢	302¢	5,600¢	2,341¢
($0.05)	**($0.35)**	**($4.26)**	**($3.02)**	**($56.00)**	**($23.41)**

Write *decimal point* on the board. Make sure the students understand that the decimal point separates the dollars from the cents. It separates the dollars from the tenths and hundredths of a dollar.

Work with the students to change the problems they multiplied in the Motivation activity into money problems. **(16 × $0.27 = $4.32; 54 × $3.45 = $186.30; 34 × $18.45 = $627.30)**

Write the terms *multistep* and *multistep problem* on the board and read them aloud. Separate the word *multistep* into *multi* and *step*. Ask students to define *step* (**"one part of a job," "one in a series of actions," and so on**). If necessary, draw a simple staircase on the board. Relate each step on the staircase as a step in a familiar task, such as brushing one's teeth. Then draw attention to the prefix *multi-*.

Lead students to understand that it means "many," or "more than one." Therefore, a *multistep problem* is a problem that has more than one step. Write these problems on the board.

$3 \times 4 = n$ $\qquad$ $3 \times (7 + 1) = m$

Lead students to understand why the second problem is a *multistep problem*. Point out that word problems can also be *multistep problems*. Write these problems on the board or read them aloud.

Matt has 14 boxes of pencils. Each box holds 8 pencils. How many pencils does Matt have? (**112 pencils**)

Matt had 14 boxes of pencils, but he gave 5 boxes away. If each box holds 8 pencils, how many pencils does Matt have left? (**72 pencils**)

Work with students to solve the problems. Then lead them to understand why the second problem is a *multistep problem*.

Guided Instruction

Write the following multiplication problems on the board. Work with students to estimate and then find the product. Use the activity to reinforce the placement and meaning of the decimal point.

$4.76	$567.23	$903.87	$503
× 34	× 45	× 34	× 23
(**$161.84**)	(**$25,525.35**)	(**$30,731.58**)	(**$11,569**)

Write the following word problem on the board and work with students to solve it. Guide students in understanding that the problem has multiple steps, and help them decide which step should be done first.

Jim and Molly went to the store. Jim bought 3 magazines at $1.59 each, and Molly bought 4 greeting cards at $1.27 each. How much more money did Molly spend than Jim? (**$0.31 more**)

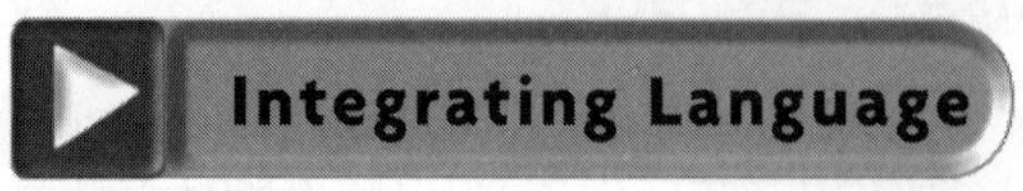

Integrating Language

Have students use the Chapter 12 Worksheet to review and practice what they have learned. You might model the process by working with students to solve the first problem orally. After students have completed their independent work, measure comprehension by checking and discussing their answers.

Name ______________________________

Multiply by 2-Digit Numbers

Find the product. Estimate to check.

1. \$5.21 × 34

\$177.14

2. \$784.09 × 63

\$49,397.67

3. \$300.76 × 76

\$22,857.76

4. \$802 × 12

\$9,624

5. \$2,987.12 × 61

\$182,214.32

6. \$502.01 × 11

\$5,522.11

Solve. Show your work in the spaces provided.

7. Dr. Sanchez bought 4 cans of soup for \$1.65 each and 3 cans of tuna for \$1.89 each. How much did she spend in all?

\$12.27

4 × \$1.65 = \$6.60; 3 × \$1.89 = \$5.67
\$6.60 + \$5.67 = \$12.27

8. Barbara usually buys VitaBlend cereal for \$3.29 a box. Last week, another brand, SilvaPop, was on sale for \$2.97. If Barbara buys 3 boxes of SilvaPop instead of 3 boxes of VitaBlend, how much money will she save?

\$0.96

3 × \$3.29 = \$9.87
3 × \$2.97 = \$8.91
\$9.87 − \$8.91 = \$0.96

Understand Division

HANDS-ON DEMONSTRATION: Have students use base-ten blocks to build models for the following expressions:

$12 \div 3$

3×4

Have volunteers explain how the expressions are related. Repeat the process with other expressions. Remind students or lead them to understand that multiplication and division are inverse operations. You may also wish to review basic division facts, the operation sign, and the terms *dividend*, *divisor*, and *quotient*.

Materials: base-ten blocks, construction paper, Chapter 13 Worksheet

Concept Vocabulary: *left over, remainder, compare, bring down*

Write the terms *left over* and *remainder* on the board and read them aloud. Explain that *left over* means "extra." Then write the following division problem on the board:

$5\overline{)37}$

Use base-ten blocks to show 37 as 3 tens 7 ones. Then ask a student to draw 5 loops on construction paper. Have students help you make 5 equal groups. Ask students *How many are left over?* Point out that in division problems, the amount left over is called the *remainder*.

Demonstrate the meanings of *compare* and the idiom *bring down*. On the board, write the steps in the order of division and the following problem:

divide
multiply
subtract
compare
bring down

$4\overline{)261}$

Demonstrate how to use the steps to solve the problem. Divide 26 by 4; multiply 6 times 4; subtract 24 from 26; *compare* 2 and the divisor 4. Since the remainder is less than the divisor, *bring down* the 1; divide 21 by 4; multiply 5 times 4; subtract 20 from 21; *compare* 1 and the divisor 4. Since the remainder is less than the divisor, the quotient is 65 r1.

Have students work with partners. Give each set of partners a set of base-ten blocks and two or three pieces of construction paper. Then have each set of partners use the base-ten blocks and loops drawn on paper to divide a simple division expression, such as 67 ÷ 8. (Devise expressions so that each contains a remainder.) Have partners work together to divide the blocks into equal groups, and use the terms *left over* and *remainder* to describe the quotient. Then have them record the division problem in standard form (such as 8)67). Finally, have them describe how they could check to make sure their quotient is correct. Repeat until each set of partners has had the opportunity to perform the demonstration.

Provide each set of partners with another division problem, such as the following.

(8 r6)	**(4 r6)**	**(4 r5)**	**(2 r2)**
9)78	7)34	6)29	9)20

Refer partners to the five steps in the order of division written on the board. Have partners take turns going to the board and working together to solve their problem, explaining and describing aloud each step in the process.

Integrating Language

Have students use the Chapter 13 Worksheet to review and practice what they have learned. You might model the process by working with students to solve the first problem orally. After students have completed their independent work, measure comprehension by checking and discussing their answers.

Name ____________________

Understand Division

Divide. Then show the check step.

1. $6\overline{)43}$ 7 r1 Check: $7 \times 6 = 42$; $42 + 1 = 43$

2. $5\overline{)38}$ 7 r3 Check: $7 \times 5 = 35$; $35 + 3 = 38$

3. $7\overline{)58}$ 8 r2 Check: $8 \times 7 = 56$; $56 + 2 = 58$

4. $3\overline{)26}$ 8 r2 Check: $8 \times 3 = 24$; $24 + 2 = 26$

5. $2\overline{)21}$ 10 r1 Check: $10 \times 2 = 20$; $20 + 1 = 21$

6. $4\overline{)31}$ 7 r3 Check: $7 \times 4 = 28$; $28 + 3 = 31$

Draw a model, record, and solve.

7. $49 \div 4$

12 r1
$4\overline{)49}$

8. $58 \div 6$ 9 r4

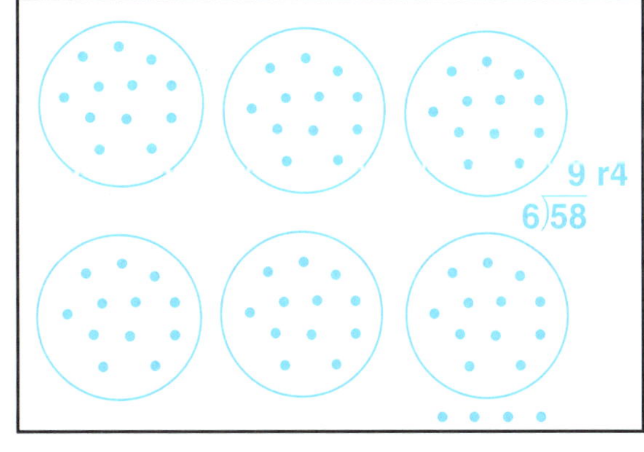

Divide and check.

9. $7\overline{)97}$ 13 r6 Check: $13 \times 7 = 91$; $91 + 6 = 97$

10. $5\overline{)26}$ 5 r1 Check: $5 \times 5 = 25$; $25 + 1 = 26$

11. $4\overline{)33}$ 8 r1 Check: $8 \times 4 = 32$; $32 + 1 = 33$

Chapter 14

Divide by 1-Digit Divisors

Motivation

HANDS-ON REVIEW: On the board, write a few simple division problems, such as

$6\overline{)420}$ $5\overline{)351}$

Using base-ten blocks, have students build models for each problem. Use the activity to review the steps in the order of division, as well as the terms *basic division facts*, *remainder*, and *pattern of zeros*.

Materials: base-ten blocks; index cards, each printed with a division problem; tables showing daily or weekly rainfalls, daily number of students attending each class, or other figures suitable for finding means

Concept Vocabulary: ***interpret, mean, average***

Write *interpret* on the board and read it aloud. Explain that *interpret* means "to explain the meaning of" or "to understand in one's own way." Present the following word problem:

> Ms. Parker has 22 boxes of pencils to distribute to the 8 classrooms in her school. How many boxes should each class receive? **(22 ÷ 8 = 2 r6)**

After students have found the quotient and the remainder, ask them to suggest how Ms. Parker should distribute the pencils in order to be fair. (**Possible answer: She should give each class 2 boxes, and save the remaining 6 boxes until a later time.**) Lead students to understand that when they thought about what to do with the remainder, they *interpreted* the remainder.

Write the terms *mean* and *average* on the board and read them aloud. Some students may be familiar with the use of *mean* to describe someone who is unkind. Explain that *mean* has a different definition for mathematics. Point out that in mathematics *mean* and *average* have similar meanings.

Explain that the *mean*, or *average*, is the number found by dividing the sum of a set of numbers by the number of addends. Use the following example to demonstrate.

Jim read three books during vacation. *All About Dogs* had 134 pages. *Deep-Sea Fishing Fun* had 249 pages. *The Stars of Ice Hockey* had 287 pages. Find the mean, or average, number of pages in the books.

$$\begin{array}{r} 134 \\ 249 \\ +\ 287 \\ \hline 670 \end{array} \qquad 3\overline{)670}$$

	223 r 1
3 goes into 6 twice	3)670
2 x 3 = 6	6
6 - 6 = 0, bring down 7	7
2 x 3 = 6	6
7 - 6 = 1, bring down 0	10
3 x 3 = 9	9
10 - 9 = 1, remainder	1

Guided Instruction

Use index cards to create a pack of "division cards." Each card should contain a division problem with a quotient and a remainder. Have students work with a partner to create a word problem for each division example. Ask volunteers from each pair to explain how they interpreted the remainder for the problem.

Guide students to find the means, or averages, in problems such as the following:

> Every day, Kay exercises. On Monday, she exercised for 35 minutes. On Tuesday, she exercised for 47 minutes. On Wednesday, she exercised for 32 minutes. What is the mean, or average, amount of minutes she exercised each day? (**38 minutes**)

Repeat with similar problems until each student has had the opportunity to solve at least one.

Integrating Language

Display charts and tables showing daily rainfall, high and low temperatures, school attendance figures, or similar figures suitable for calculating means. Have students work in small groups or with partners. Give each group or set of partners a table. Instruct them to find the mean, or average. Allow time for students to share their results, using the concept vocabulary appropriately.

Chapter 15

Divide by 2-Digit Divisors

HANDS-ON EXPERIMENT: Provide students with a number line like the one shown below, and the following clues. Have students use the clues to solve the puzzle.

1. Write a *T* above a number that is less than 7.
2. Write a *T* above a number that is more than 9.
3. Write a *Q* above a number that is less than 4.
4. Write an *A* above a number that is less than 2.
5. Write an *N* above a number that is more than 8.
6. Write an *O* above a number that is less than 6.
7. Write a *U* above a number that is less than 5.
8. Write an *I* above a number that is more than 6.
9. Write an *E* above a number that is more than 7.

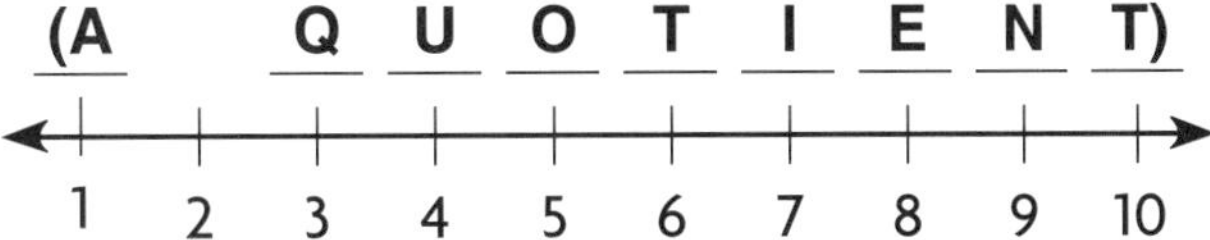

Concept Vocabulary: *increase, decrease, too high, too low, just right*

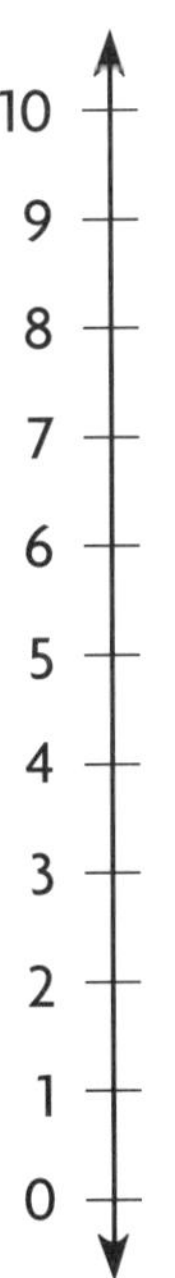

Write all vocabulary terms on the board and read them aloud. Write the number 5 on the board. Using vertical arrows pointing up and down, create a vertical number line, asking each student to place a number above or below 5 on the scale.

Use the scale to explain the meanings of *increase* and *decrease*. If possible, reinforce the concepts by displaying a thermometer. Elicit from students that when the weather gets warmer, the temperature *increases*, and when the weather turns colder, the temperature *decreases*.

Then pick a number on the number scale as a "secret number." Invite students to guess it. Answer each incorrect guess *too high* or *too low*, leading students to understand the meanings through the relative values of the numbers. Then reward the correct guess by saying *just right*, leading students to understand that this American idiom means "exact answer."

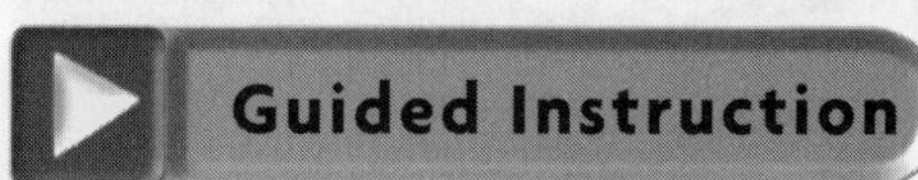

Write the expression 164 ÷ 43 on the board. Point out that you can begin to solve this division problem by estimating the quotient. Have students round the divisor and the dividend to the greatest place value or to the nearest compatible number. Write on the board 160 ÷ 40. Guide students to use basic division facts to find the quotient (**4**). Point out that this is an estimated quotient for the problem 164 ÷ 43. Then write on the board:

$43\overline{)164}$

Work with students to try the estimate. Point out that since 172 (4 × 43) is greater than 164, the estimate of 4 is *too high*. Lead students to understand that they must *decrease* the estimate one step to 3. Now work with students to try the estimate of 3. Point out that since 129 (3 × 43) is less than 164, it works; it is *just right*. Subtract 164 − 129, showing the remainder of 35. Elicit from students that the exact quotient is 3 r35. Have them summarize how estimating helped them decide whether their answer was reasonable, and how they used the terms *too high*, *decrease*, and *just right* during the solving process.

Repeat with similar problems, allowing each student an opportunity to assist you in estimating and solving. Have students use the terms *increase*, *decrease*, *too high*, *too low*, and *just right* whenever possible.

Integrating Language

Write a series of problems like the following on the board, or create and photocopy a worksheet. Have students work independently or with partners to decide whether each estimate is *too high*, *too low*, or *just right*. Then have them divide to find the exact quotient. Have volunteers present their findings to the class using the concept vocabulary.

$\begin{array}{r}9\\43\overline{)369}\end{array}$ **(too high; 8 r25)** $\begin{array}{r}6\\37\overline{)243}\end{array}$ **(just right; 6 r21)**

$\begin{array}{r}6\\22\overline{)131}\end{array}$ **(too high; 5 r21)** $\begin{array}{r}2\\53\overline{)211}\end{array}$ **(too low; 3 r52)**

Chapter 16

Number Theory

Motivation

HANDS-ON REVIEW: Have students work in pairs. Assign a 2-digit number, such as 12, 20, or 30, to each pair and challenge them to use arrays to show as many factors of the number as possible in a given amount of time. At the end of the timed period, have the partners write down the factors they identified. Then assign a new number to each pair and repeat the process. Discuss any strategies partners used to find factors more quickly.

Materials: Chapter 16 Worksheet

Concept Vocabulary: *composite number, prime number, prime factor*

Write the terms *composite number* and *prime number* on the board and read them aloud. Refer to one of the numbers used for the Motivation activity and ask students to identify its factors. For example, 12 has the factors 1, 2, 3, 4, 6, 12. Point out that a *composite number* has more than two factors. Therefore, since 12 has 6 factors, it is a composite number. Repeat, using the number 16. Have students name the factors and explain why it is a composite number.

Then write the number 13 on the board. Ask students to name its factors. Lead them to understand that 13 has only 2 factors—1 and 13. Point out that a *prime number* has only two factors—itself and 1. Therefore, since 13 has only 2 factors, it is a prime number. Repeat, using the number 7. Have students name the factors and explain why it is a prime number.

Write the following equation on the board: $6 \times 4 = 24$ and ask students to name its factors (**1, 2, 3, 4, 6, 8, 12, 24**). Ask them whether 24 is a composite number or a prime number. (**composite**) Then write the term *prime factor* on the board and read it aloud. Point out that any composite number can be written as a product of prime factors, which are all the prime numbers in a factor tree. To illustrate, create a factor tree for 24.

```
        24
        /\
       6 x 4        (Use any 2 factors of 24.)
      /\    \
     2 x 3 x 4      (Continue until only prime factors are left.)
    /   /   /\
   2 x 3 x 2 x 2
```

Lead students to understand that the prime factors of 24 are 2 and 3.

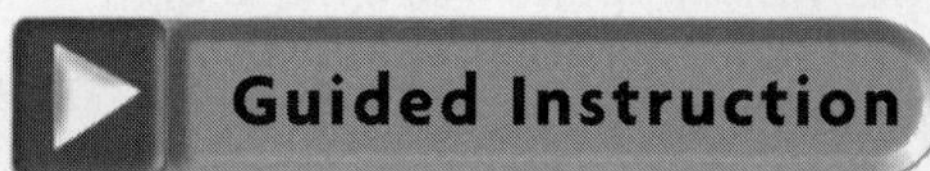

Guided Instruction

Write the numbers 17 and 18 on the chalkboard. Work with students to look for possible factors for these numbers. Lead them to determine that 17 is a prime number and 18 is a composite number. Have them explain why this is so using the guarded vocabulary. **(17 has only two factors, itself and 1, so it is a prime number. 18 has the factors 1, 2, 3, 6, 9, and 18, so it is a composite number.**) Write the number 36 on the board. Work with students to create a factor tree, and lead them to determine that the prime factors of 36 are 2 and 3 ($2 \times 2 \times 3 \times 3$). Then have students take turns determining the prime factors of various composite numbers. Close by having students explain the relationship between composite numbers and prime factors.

Integrating Language

Have students use the Chapter 16 Worksheet to review and practice what they have learned. You might model the process by working with students to solve the first problem orally. After students have completed their independent work, measure comprehension by checking and discussing their answers.

Number Theory

List as many factors as you can for each number.

1. 15 1, 3, 5, 15

2. 28 1, 2, 4, 7, 14, 28

3. 23 1, 23

4. 32 1, 2, 4, 8, 16, 32

5. Which number or numbers above (15, 28, 23, 32) are *prime numbers*?

   23

6. What is a prime number?

   any number that has only two factors—itself and 1

7. Which number or numbers above (15, 28, 23, 32) are *composite numbers*?

   15, 28, 32

8. What is a composite number?

   any number that has more than two factors

Circle *prime* or *composite* for each number.

9. 13 prime (circled) composite

10. 33 prime composite (circled)

11. 45 prime composite (circled)

12. 19 prime (circled) composite

Complete the factor tree to find the prime factors of the number.

13. 10
/ \
2 x 5

Prime factors: 2, 5

14. 48
/ \
6 x 8
2 x 3 x 2 x 2 x 2

Prime factors: 2, 3

15. 18
/ \
6 x 3 or 2 x 9
2 x 3 x 3

Prime factors: 2, 3

16. 50
/ \
25 x 2 or 10 x 5
5 x 5 x 2

Prime factors: 2, 5

17. 27
/ \
9 x 3
3 x 3 x 3

Prime factors: 3

18. 54
/ \
9 x 6 or 27 x 2
3 x 3 x 2 x 3

Prime factors: 2, 3

Chapter 17

Lines, Rays, and Angles

HANDS-ON REVIEW: Display a square, a right triangle, a parallelogram containing acute and obtuse angles, and a circle. Have students identify sides and angles. Then remind them, if necessary, what a right angle is. Have them point out the right angles in the square and right triangle. Finally, have them use the triangle and parallelogram to point out angles that are smaller and greater than right angles.

Materials: plane figures (2 squares of different sizes, 2 right triangles of the same size, parallelogram, circle) cut from construction paper; colored chalk; Chapter 17 Worksheet

Concept Vocabulary: ***acute, obtuse, point, endpoint, parallel, perpendicular, congruent, similar***

Write the terms *acute* and *obtuse* on the board and read them aloud. Use the triangle and parallelogram to demonstrate that angles smaller than right angles are called *acute*, and angles larger than right angles are called *obtuse*. Have volunteers come to the board to draw examples of acute, right, and obtuse angles, labeling them with letters, such as:

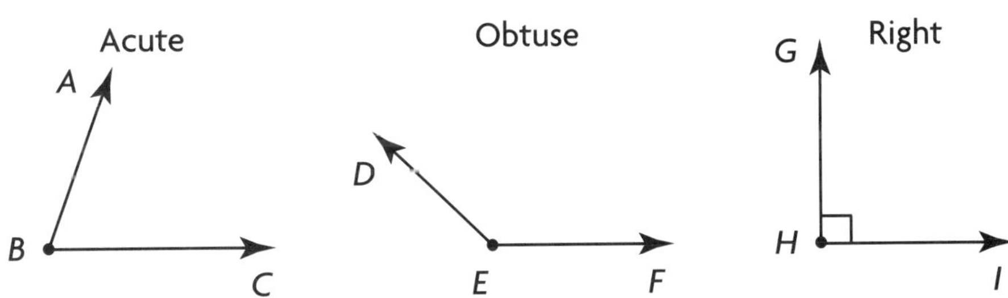

Write the terms *point* and *endpoint* on the board and read them aloud. Explain that the math term *point* names a specific location on an object or in space. As an example, draw a dot on the board and label it *A*. Explain that Point *A* is a location on the surface of the board. If necessary, review the difference between lines, line segments, and rays, drawing examples on the board as follows:

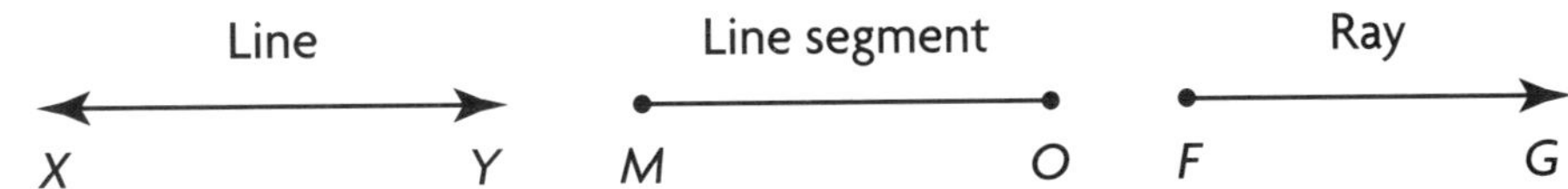

Then draw attention to line segment *MO*. Label another point on the line as *D*. Point out to students that when points appear at the ends of line segments, they are called *endpoints*. Ask students to use the letters to name the endpoints of the line segment on the board.

Write the terms *parallel* and *perpendicular* on the board and read them aloud. Draw a set of each type of lines on the board. Use the positions of the lines, and the formation of right angles, to demonstrate the differences. Ask students to name examples of parallel and perpendicular lines in the classroom. Use the square, parallelogram, and triangle to point out the presence and absence of parallel lines in various plane figures.

Write the terms *congruent* and *similar* on the board and read them aloud. Then display the two squares of different sizes and two right triangles of the same size. Discuss with students how the members of each pair are alike and different, leading them to understand that because the squares have the same shape but different sizes, they are *similar*, and that because the right triangles have the same shape and size, they are *congruent*. Then flip one of the triangles. Lead students to understand that although the triangles are now in different positions, their congruency remains because their identical sizes and shapes remain the same.

Guided Instruction

On the board, use white chalk to draw several lines, line segments, rays, squares, rectangles, right triangles, parallelograms, parallel lines, and perpendicular lines. Include examples of congruent and similar figures. Label each drawing with letters, as in line *XY*. Have students take turns coming to the board to use the colored chalk to circle or emphasize a feature on cue. For example, use such cues as *I am triangle MLP. With red chalk, place point D on side ML;* and *I am triangle MLP. With blue chalk, circle any of my angles that is acute.* Repeat until students have each had two or three opportunities to respond.

Integrating Language

Have students use the Chapter 17 Worksheet to review and practice what they have learned. After students have completed their independent work, measure comprehension by checking and discussing their answers.

Name ______________________

Lines, Rays, and Angles

Choose a term from the box to label each drawing.

perpendicular lines	similar figures
parallel lines	congruent figures
line segment	acute angle
ray	obtuse angle

1. 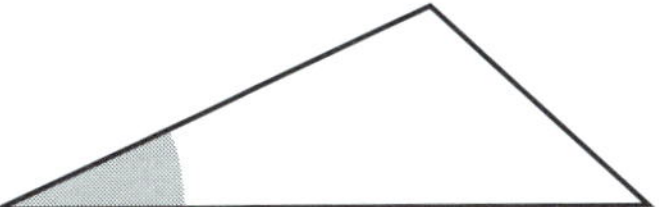

acute angle

2.  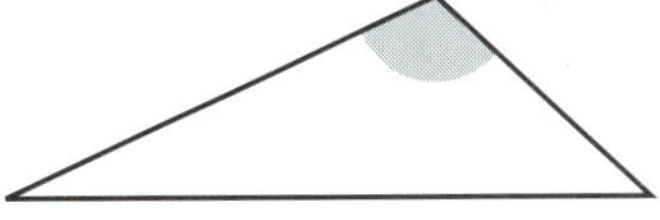

obtuse angle

3.

parallel lines

4. 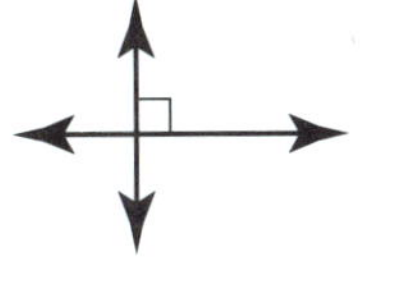

perpendicular lines

5. 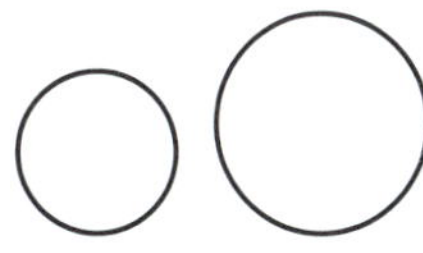

similar figures

6. 

congruent figures

7. 

ray

8. 

line segment

Draw and label an example of each. Check students' drawings.

9. right angle ABC

10. point M

11. line $\overleftrightarrow{NK}$

12. parallel lines $\overleftrightarrow{AB}$ and $\overleftrightarrow{NT}$

Chapter 18

Plane Figures

Motivation

MENTAL ACTIVITY: On the chalkboard draw an open plane figure, an irregular closed figure, and a circle. Work with the students to label the figures and discuss how the figures are alike and how they are different. **(All 3 are plane figures because they are drawn on a flat surface. The second and third figures are closed figures, but a circle is made up of points that are the same distance from its center.)**

Work with the students to draw and label the radius, a chord, and the diameter of the circle and to define each.
(radius: line segment with one endpoint at the center of the circle and the other endpoint on the circle; chord: line segment with both endpoints on the circle; diameter: chord that passes through the center of the circle)

Materials: Chapter 18 Worksheet

Concept Vocabulary: ***closed plane figure, circle, radius, diameter, chord, polygon, triangle, pentagon, hexagon, octagon, quadrilateral, trapezoid, parallelogram, rhombus, rectangle, square***

On the chalkboard write *polygon* and discuss its meaning. **(a closed plane figure with straight sides)**

Say *triangle*. Have a student write the word on the chalkboard and draw the figure. Have another student say what a triangle is. **(A triangle is a polygon with 3 sides.)**
Continue in this way with the other concept vocabulary.
(pentagon: polygon with 5 sides;
hexagon: polygon with 6 sides;
octagon: polygon with 8 sides;
quadrilateral: polygon with 4 sides;
trapezoid: quadrilateral with 2 pairs of parallel sides;
parallelogram: quadrilateral with 2 pairs of parallel sides, 2 pairs of equal sides;
rhombus: a parallelogram with 4 equal sides;
rectangle: a parallelogram with 4 equal angles;
square: a parallelogram with 4 equal sides and 4 equal angles;

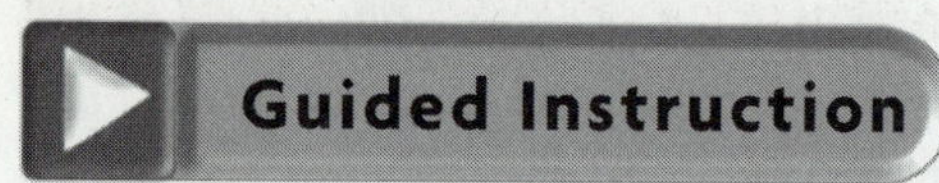

Guided Instruction

Copy the chart below on the board. Guide students in applying their knowledge of the concept vocabulary to complete it.

	Draw the figure	Closed plane figure	polygon	quadrilateral	parallelogram	rhombus	rectangle	square
Circle		yes	no	no	no	no	no	no
Triangle		yes	yes	no	no	no	no	no
Pentagon		yes	yes	no	no	no	no	no
Hexagon		yes	yes	no	no	no	no	no
Octagon		yes	yes	no	no	no	no	no
Quadrilateral		yes	yes	—	no	no	no	no
Trapezoid		yes	yes	yes	no	no	no	no
Pallelogram		yes	yes	yes	—	no	no	no
Rhombus		yes	yes	yes	yes	—	no	no
Rectangle		yes	yes	yes	yes	no	—	no
Square		yes	yes	yes	yes	yes	yes	—

Integrating Language

Name one of the plane figures in the chart, such as circle. Have students say what the figure is and why it does or does not have some of the names.

A circle is a closed plane figure, but it is not a polygon because it does not have straight sides. It is not a quadrilateral because it does not have 4 sides. It is not a parallelogram because it does not have opposite sides that are equal and parallel. It is not a rhombus because it does not have 4 equal sides and 2 pairs of equal angles, and so on.

Continue with the other figures. Remind students to use the concept vocabulary in their discussion.

Have students complete the Chapter 18 Worksheet. Then measure their comprehension by checking and discussing their answers.

Plane Figures

Circle the name of the shape to solve each riddle.
Draw a picture of the shape.

1. I am a closed figure but I am not a polygon. I have many chords. Who am I?

circle rhombus

2. I am a polygon with more sides than a triangle, but fewer sides than a pentagon. Who am I?

quadrilateral hexagon

3. I am a quadrilateral but I am not a parallelogram. Who am I?

rectangle trapezoid

4. I am both a rectangle and a rhombus. Who am I?

square triangle

5. I am a polygon with twice as many sides as a quadrilateral. Who am I?

pentagon octagon

6. I am a quadrilateral with 2 pairs of parallel sides. Who am I?

triangle parallelogram

7. I am a parallelogram with all equal sides. Who am I?

rhombus hexagon

8. I am a parallelogram with all equal angles. Who am I?

trapezoid square

9. I am a polygon with 2 more sides than a quadrilateral. Who am I?

trapezoid hexagon

10. I am a closed figure. I am not a polygon. Who am I?

quadrilateral circle

Chapter 19

Motion Geometry

ACTIVITY: Have the students begin to put the puzzle together. Discuss the movements they make with the pieces, such as sliding along a straight line, turning the puzzle piece around a point, or flipping a puzzle piece right side up, like flipping over a line.

Materials: jigsaw puzzle, checker board, Chapter 19 Worksheet

Write the word *transformation* on the board. Tell the students that a transformation is the movement of a plane figure. They were transforming the puzzle pieces as they moved them. They were transforming them in three ways.

1. Slide or *translation* when they moved a figure to a new place along a straight line.
2. Flip or *reflection* when they flipped the puzzle piece over a line.
3. Turn or *rotation* when they moved the figure around a point.

Discuss how the puzzle pieces were like closed figures that covered a surface with no gaps and no overlaps. Some puzzles have a repeating pattern. Then we would say the pieces *tessellate* and the result is a *tessellation*.

Show the students the checkerboard. Have them name the figures used and the pattern. **(black square, red square)** Make sure that they notice that there are no gaps or overlaps. They can see that squares tessellate and a checkerboard is an example of a tessellation.

Write the words *similar* and *congruent*. Discuss their meanings. Congruent figures have the same shape and size. Similar figures have the same shape but have different sizes. Remind students that figures do not have to be in the same position to be congruent or similar.

Draw these rectangles on the board. Have the students say which are congruent and which are similar. **(A and C are congruent; B is similar to both A and C.)**

A B C

Guided Instruction

Work with the students to fill in this chart on the board. Have one student write the names of the three transformations; have another student write the meanings; and another student draw examples. Repeat with the other transformations.

Transformations		
Translation	Move along a straight line	
Reflection	Flip over a line	
Rotation	Turn around a point	

Ask the students what other vocabulary word begins with the letter *T*. **(tessellation)** Have one of the students give the meaning of *tessellation*. Ask whether the squares on the checkerboard are similar or congruent. **(congruent)**

Discuss how a puzzle's difficulty would change if the puzzle had some congruent pieces. **(more difficult to put together, because while some pieces would fit each other, those pieces may be in the wrong locations)**

Integrating Language

Have the children complete the Chapter 19 Worksheet by themselves.

Then have the children take turns explaining their answers using the concept vocabulary.

Name ______________________________

Motion Geometry

Circle the correct answer.

1. Figures that have the same shape but not the same size are _____.

   congruent translation similar

2. A pattern of polygons that completely cover a surface without overlapping is a _____.

   transformation tessellation translation

3. The movement of a plane figure is called a _____.

   transformation tessellation translation

4. Figures that are the same size and the same shape are _____.

   rotation congruent similar

5. Plane figures that are moved along a straight line are _____.

   translated rotated reflected

6. Plane figures that are flipped to a new position are _____.

   translated rotated reflected

7. Plane figures that are turned around a point are _____.

   translated rotated reflected

Draw an example of each.

Similar figures	Congruent figures	Reflection	Translation	Rotation

Algebra: Explore Negative Numbers and Graphing

GAME: Tell students that they will play a game called "Cold—Warm—Hot." On the board draw a line resembling a number line, but write *cold* at the "lowest" end, *warm* at the midpoint, and *hot* at the "highest" end. Have students take turns naming things that are very cold, slightly cold, warm, slightly hot, and very hot. Write each item at the appropriate place on the line. Emphasize that if this were a number line, the number 1 might represent very cold and the number 10 might represent very hot.

Materials: Fahrenheit and Celsius thermometers, encyclopedia or almanac, number line showing $^{-}10$ to 10, Chapter 20 Worksheet

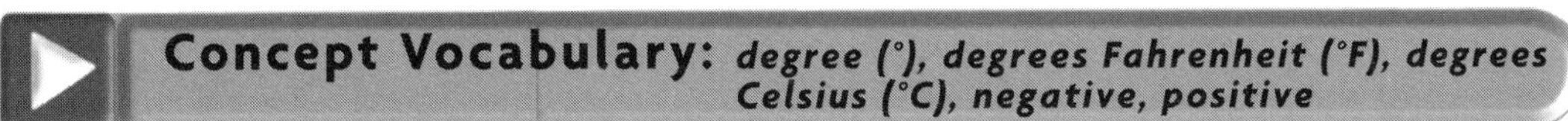

Write the terms, symbols, and abbreviations *degree (°), degrees Fahrenheit (°F),* and *degrees Celsius (°C)* on the board, read the terms aloud, and explain the symbol and abbreviations. Remind students that they learned a meaning for *degree* when they were studying about angles (the unit by which angles are measured). Point out that *degree* has another meaning, which is the unit by which temperature is measured. Refer to the game line from the Motivation activity, pointing out that the temperature of very cold items would be a low number of degrees, and the temperature of very hot items would be a high number of degrees.

Display the Fahrenheit and Celsius thermometers, identify them as customary and metric measurement tools, and discuss how they are alike and different. Point out the points at which water boils and freezes on each, reinforcing the concept of low numbers of degrees and high numbers of degrees. Have students read the thermometers to tell what each one registers for room temperature. Have them use the words *degrees, Fahrenheit,* and *Celsius* in their responses.

Write the terms *negative* and *positive* on the board and read them aloud. Point out that on warm days, the temperature rises well above zero, and on very cold days, the temperature may go below zero. Point out the markings for positive and negative degrees on the thermometers. Identify numbers above zero as *positive numbers* and numbers below zero as *negative numbers*. Lead students to understand that temperatures below zero can be written as, for example, *$^{-}10^{\circ}$* or *ten below zero*. Stress that the minus sign ($-$) is used to show that a number is negative.

Guided Instruction

Have students take turns naming a country or state that they have studied in social studies. Have them use the almanac or encyclopedia to find the average annual high and low temperatures of each country or state. Have each student present his or her findings orally, using the terms *degrees*, *Fahrenheit*, and *Celsius*. Then work with students to calculate the change in temperature from a region's high and low, showing them, for example, that the change between 78°F and $^{-}10$°F is 88°. Have students take turns calculating the number of degrees in various temperature changes.

Display the number line. Discuss how a number line is similar to a thermometer. (**It shows both positive and negative numbers.**) Have students take turns pointing out positive and negative numbers on the line.

Finally, use the symbols $<$ and $>$ to stress that although $5 < 8$, $^{-}5 > {}^{-}8$ because $^{-}5$ is closer to zero. If students have difficulty grasping this concept, refer to the thermometers, equating greater warmth with greater amount. ($^{-}5^{\circ}$ would be warmer than $^{-}8^{\circ}$, and it is higher, or closer to zero, on the thermometer; similarly, $^{-}5$ is greater than $^{-}8$, and it is closer to zero on the number line.) Repeat until all students have had a turn to use $<$ and $>$ to compare a pair of negative numbers.

Integrating Language

Have students use the Chapter 20 Worksheet to review and practice what they have learned. After students have completed their independent work, measure comprehension by checking and discussing their answers.

Name ______________________________

Algebra: Explore Negative Numbers and Graphing

Use the words and abbreviations in the box to complete each sentence.

Fahrenheit (°F)	Celsius (°C)

1. Degrees **Fahrenheit (°F)** are customary units for measuring temperature.

2. Degrees Celsius (°C) are metric units for measuring temperature.

Compare. Write $<$, $>$, or $=$ in each ◯.

3. $^{-}10$°F ◯ 10°F $<$
4. 32°F ◯ 0°C $=$
5. 3°C ◯ $^{-}5$°C $>$
6. $^{-}18$°F ◯ $^{-}6$°F $<$

7. Fill in the missing numbers on the number line.

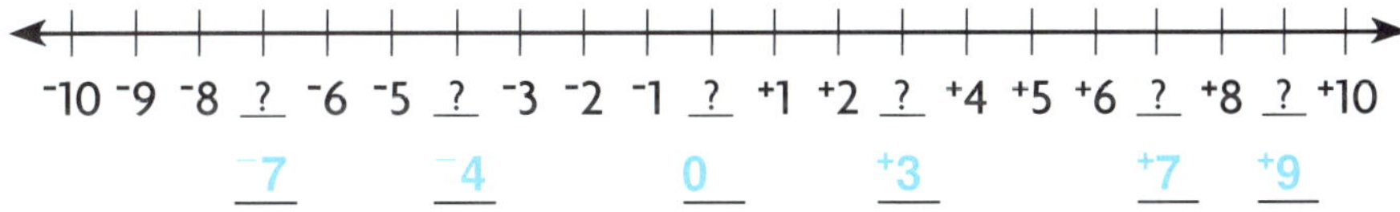

8. Which of the numbers that you wrote in Exercise 7 are *negative*? $^{-}7$ and $^{-}4$

Compare. Write $<$, $>$, or $=$ in each ◯. Use the number line for extra help.

9. $^{-}6$ ◯ $^{+}4$ $<$
10. $^{-}2$ ◯ $^{+}2$ $<$
11. $^{-}9$ ◯ $^{-}2$ $<$
12. $^{+}8$ ◯ $^{-}9$ $>$

Chapter 21

Understand Fractions

Motivation

HANDS-ON DEMONSTRATION: Use fraction tiles to represent $\frac{1}{2}$, both as part of a whole and as part of a group.

Ask students to name the fraction represented by each model. Write the fraction on the board. Remind students that a fraction is a number that can name two different things: a part of a whole and a part of a group. Repeat, creating models to represent $\frac{1}{4}$, $\frac{1}{3}$, and so on. Use the demonstrations to review the concept of fractions.

Materials: rainbow fraction tiles; play money, coins and bills; Chapter 21 Worksheet

Concept Vocabulary: *numerator, denominator, equivalent, mixed number*

Write the terms *numerator* and *denominator* on the board and read them aloud.

Write several fractions on the board, such as $\frac{3}{5}$, $\frac{1}{4}$, and $\frac{2}{9}$. Explain that the *numerator* is the top number in a fraction, while the *denominator* is the bottom number. Lead students to identify the numerator and the denominator in each fraction, and to read the fraction aloud properly (three fifths, one fourth, two ninths), using the numerator and denominator.

Write the term *equivalent* on the board and read it aloud. Remind students that objects that are *equivalent* are equal. As an example, display two nickels and one dime of play money. Lead students to understand that they are equivalent amounts of money. Ask students to make other sets of coins with equivalent values. Then extend *equivalent* to *equivalent fractions*. Lead students to understand that equivalent fractions have equal values. Use fraction tiles to demonstrate that $\frac{1}{2}$, $\frac{2}{4}$, and $\frac{3}{6}$ are equivalent fractions.

Write the term *mixed number* on the board and read it aloud. Use fraction tiles to make a model that represents $1\frac{1}{2}$ and write the mixed number on the board. Define *mixed number* as a number that is made up of a whole number and a fraction. Have students suggest other examples of mixed numbers.

Guided Instruction

Have students take turns coming to the board to write fractions. Give them such cues as *three fourths*. After each student writes the fraction correctly, have him or her identify the numerator and the denominator.

Distribute fraction tiles. Have students take turns experimenting with the tiles to build as many equivalent fractions as they can. Start each student off with a fraction in simplest form, such as $\frac{1}{2}$, $\frac{1}{3}$, $\frac{1}{4}$, and so on. Challenge students to build equivalents. Provide time for each student to identify his or her set of equivalent fractions.

Have students use fraction tiles to build models of mixed numbers. Give them such cues as *three and four ninths*. After each model is built, ask the student to write the mixed number. Repeat until each student has had at least one turn.

Integrating Language

Have students use Chapter 21 Worksheet to review and practice what they have learned. You might model the process by working with students to solve the first problem orally. After students have completed their independent work, measure comprehension by checking and discussing their answers.

Name ______________________________

Understand Fractions

1. Which number is the denominator in the fraction $\frac{7}{8}$? **8**

2. Which number is the numerator in the fraction $\frac{5}{16}$? 5

Write the fraction or mixed number for the shaded part.

3. 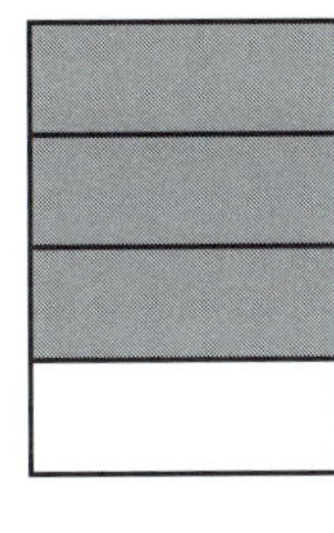

$\frac{3}{4}$

4. 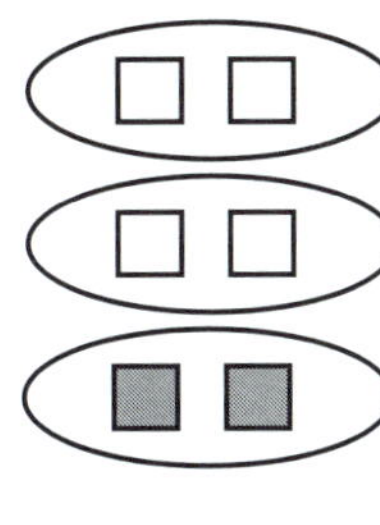

$\frac{1}{3}$

5. 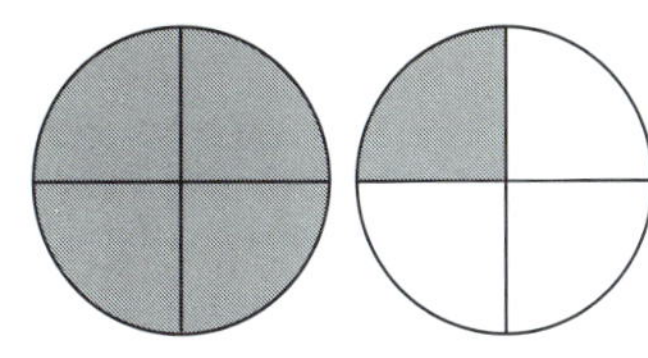

$1\frac{1}{4}$

In each set of fractions, circle the equivalent fractions.

6. $\frac{1}{2}$ $\frac{3}{6}$ $\frac{5}{6}$ $\frac{7}{10}$ $\frac{4}{8}$

7. $\frac{3}{4}$ $\frac{7}{8}$ $\frac{9}{12}$ $\frac{9}{10}$ $\frac{6}{8}$

8. $\frac{6}{7}$ $\frac{5}{6}$ $\frac{10}{12}$ $\frac{10}{14}$ $\frac{4}{7}$

Write the fraction or mixed number.

9. five eighths $\frac{5}{8}$

10. eight thirteenths $\frac{8}{13}$

11. fifteen and two thirds $15\frac{2}{3}$

12. twenty-seven and nine tenths $27\frac{9}{10}$

Chapter 22

Add and Subtract Fractions and Mixed Numbers

Motivation

HANDS-ON REVIEW: Have students use rainbow fraction tiles to make fraction models showing a variety of addition and subtraction problems. For example, have students show how they would represent $\frac{1}{3} + \frac{2}{3}$, $\frac{3}{4} + \frac{2}{4}$, $\frac{5}{6} - \frac{1}{6}$, and $\frac{2}{3} - \frac{1}{3}$. Then ask students to make a model for $\frac{3}{4} + \frac{1}{2}$. Ask how making this model differs from making the others. Lead students to understand that the last model they made is the same as the one for $\frac{3}{4} + \frac{2}{4}$.

Materials: rainbow fraction tiles

Concept Vocabulary: *like fractions, unlike fractions*

Write the term *like fractions* on the board and read it aloud. Use examples such as $\frac{2}{3}$ and $\frac{1}{3}$ to explain that *like fractions* have the same denominator. Have each student suggest a pair of like fractions.

Write the term *unlike fractions* on the board and read it aloud. Point out the prefix *un-*, explaining that it often means "not." Therefore, *unlike fractions* are "not like" each other. They have different denominators. Write a pair of fractions such as $\frac{1}{6}$ and $\frac{1}{2}$ on the board as an example. Have each student suggest another pair of unlike fractions.

Guided Instruction

On the board, write a series of addition and subtraction problems involving like fractions. For example:

$\frac{1}{\boxed{3}} + \frac{1}{\boxed{3}} =$ $\quad$ $\frac{1}{4} + \frac{2}{4} =$ $\quad$ $\frac{1}{8} + \frac{5}{8} =$

$\frac{7}{8} - \frac{3}{8} =$ $\quad$ $\frac{6}{7} - \frac{3}{7} =$ $\quad$ $\frac{5}{6} - \frac{1}{6} =$

Elicit from students that each of these addition and subtraction problems contains a pair of *like fractions*, because each pair contains the same denominator. Work with students to solve each problem. Begin by modeling each problem with rainbow fraction tiles, leading students to understand that when the denominators are the same, the problem is solved by adding or subtracting the numerators. Repeat, having students take turns solving a problem independently. Provide at least one addition and one subtraction problem for each student.

Repeat the activity with unlike fractions, writing such problems as the following on the board:

$\frac{\boxed{1}}{4} + \frac{\boxed{1}}{2} =$ $\qquad \frac{1}{3} + \frac{1}{4} =$ $\qquad \frac{2}{3} + \frac{1}{2} =$

$\frac{5}{8} - \frac{1}{4} =$ $\qquad \frac{7}{8} - \frac{1}{2} =$ $\qquad \frac{3}{4} - \frac{1}{3} =$

Elicit from students that each of these addition and subtraction problems contains a pair of *unlike fractions*, because the fraction in each pair has a different denominator. Work with students to solve each problem. Begin by modeling the problem with rainbow fraction tiles, leading students to understand that when the denominators are different, the problem is solved by first finding equivalent fractions with like denominators. Then, add or subtract the numerators. Finally, if necessary, reduce the answer fraction to its simplest form. Repeat, having students take turns solving a problem independently. Provide at least one addition and one subtraction problem for each student.

Integrating Language

Have students work with partners to create Fraction Challenge Sheets for another set of partners to solve. Instruct them to create addition and subtraction problems containing a balance of *like fractions* and *unlike fractions*. After partners have completed their Fraction Challenge Sheets, collect and check the sheets for accuracy. Then have partners exchange papers with other partners and work together to solve the problems. Provide time for review of their work and to reinforce the terms *like* and *unlike fractions*.

Chapter 23

Outcomes and Probability

HANDS-ON EXPERIMENT: Provide each student with two red counters. Give them the following directions:

- Hold up one red counter.
- Hold up two red counters.
- Hold up three red counters.
- Hold up a blue counter.

Elicit that students were able to follow the first two directions, but could not follow the last two because the required counters were not available to them.

Materials: play money coins, two-color counters, spinners, Chapter 23 Worksheet

Concept Vocabulary: ***certain, possible, impossible, likely, unlikely, equally likely***

Write *certain*, *possible*, *impossible*, *likely*, *unlikely*, and *equally likely* on the board. Read the words aloud. Use the words *certain* and *impossible* in sentences such as,

> I have five pennies in a bag. I take out one coin. It is *certain* to be a penny.

> I have five pennies in a bag. I take out one coin. It is *impossible* that it will be a nickel.

Lead students to understand that the first outcome is certain because all possible picks are pennies, and that the second outcome is impossible because all possible picks are pennies. Explain that an event that is *certain* will always occur, and an event that is *impossible* will never occur.

Draw attention to the term *possible*. Explain that it describes an event that may or may not happen. For example,

> I have three pennies and two nickels in a bag. I take out one coin. It is *possible* that it will be a nickel.

Lead students to understand that the outcome is possible because the bag contains both pennies and nickels.

Next, define *likely* and *unlikely*, pointing out that a likely event is one that will probably happen, whereas an unlikely event is one that will probably *not* happen. For example,

> I have four pennies and one nickel in a bag. I take out one coin. It is *likely* that it will be a penny. It is *unlikely* that it will be a nickel.

Lead students to understand that the first outcome is likely because you have more pennies than nickels. The second outcome is unlikely, although possible.

Then focus on the concept of *equally likely*, saying:

> I have three pennies and three nickels in a bag. I take out one coin. It is *equally likely* that it will be a penny or a nickel.

Lead students to understand that the outcomes are equally likely because you have the same number of each coin.

Guided Instruction

Assemble a pile of play coins on a table. The pile should contain an equal amount of nickels and dimes, twice as many pennies, and no quarters. Have students examine the pile of coins. Then ask questions such as the following to elicit use of the vocabulary terms in their responses.

- What are my chances of pulling a quarter from this pile of coins? (**impossible**)
- What are my chances of pulling a penny, nickel, or dime from this pile of coins? (**possible**)
- What are my chances of pulling a penny? (**likely**)
- If I took all the pennies away, would I have an equal chance of pulling a nickel and a dime? Why or why not? What are such chances called? (**yes; same number of nickels as dimes; equally likely**)

If time allows, repeat with similar activities involving spinners and two-color counters, allowing each student one or more chances to differentiate among outcomes that are *certain*, *possible*, *impossible*, *likely*, *unlikely*, and *equally likely*.

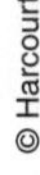

Integrating Language

Have students use the Chapter 23 Worksheet to review and practice what they have learned. After students have completed their independent work, measure comprehension by checking and discussing their answers.

Outcomes and Probability

Write *certain*, *possible*, *impossible*, *likely*, or *unlikely* to describe each event.

1. pulling a red cube from a bag containing 8 red cubes and 2 yellow cubes likely

2. rolling an even number on a number cube numbered 1 to 6 possible

3. spinning an even number on a 6-part spinner labeled 1, 5, 7, 8, 11, 13 unlikely

4. pulling a green marble from a bag containing 18 blue marbles, 7 yellow marbles, and 6 white marbles impossible

5. tossing a coin and getting either heads or tails certain

6. rolling a number greater than 2 on a number cube numbered 1 to 6 likely

Maria has 4 green pencils and 4 red pencils in her desk drawer. Without looking into the drawer, she reaches in to pick a pencil.

7. Describe an impossible outcome.

Possible answer: She picks a black pencil.

8. Describe an equally likely outcome.

Possible answer: She picks a green pencil or a red pencil.

Chapter 24

Customary Measurement

Motivation

HANDS-ON EXPERIMENT: Provide each student with a customary ruler. Review the terms *inch* and *foot*. (You may want to point out that the measurement *foot* was so named because it is about the length of a man's foot.) Then provide each student with an item to measure to the nearest inch.

Materials: rulers; yardstick; clear glass or plastic 1-cup, 2-cup, and 1-quart graduated measuring containers; 2 clear plastic gallon jugs—1 empty and 1 filled with water; scale; Chapter 24 Worksheet

Concept Vocabulary: ***linear units, capacity, cup, weight, pound (lb)***

Write the term *linear units* on the board and read it aloud. Then use a yardstick and your desk or a classroom table to demonstrate that you can measure its length, its height, and its width. Stress that inches, feet, yards, and miles are all *linear units*. Write each term on the board under *linear units*.

Write the terms *capacity* and *cup* on the board and read them aloud. Display the measuring cups and the gallon jug filled with water. Lead students to understand that *capacity* is a measurement of the amount a container can hold when it is full. Use the jug of water as an example, pointing out that its capacity is one gallon. Then explain that only measuring cups are a standardized size. Therefore, other types of cups are not accurate measuring devices. Elicit examples such as the standard carton of milk sold in the cafeteria holds 1 cup; cartons of milk and orange juice are sold in 1-quart, 2-quart, and 1-gallon capacities; and so on.

Write the terms *weight* and *pound (lb)* on the board and read them aloud. Display the scale. Lead students to understand that *weight* is a measure of how heavy an object is, and that weight can be measured in ounces, pounds, and tons. As an example, weigh various classroom objects, having students tell how much each one weighs. Give examples of things that weigh one or more tons. Point out the unusual abbreviation *(lb)* that is used to signify pounds.

Guided Instruction

Write the outline of the following chart on the board. (You might also prepare the outline on a sheet of paper and distribute photocopies for students to fill in and keep for reference and review.)

Customary Measurement

Types of Measurement	Units of Measurement/Equivalents	
Linear	inch (in) foot (ft) yard (yd) mile (mi)	12 inches = 1 foot 3 feet = 1 yard 1,760 yd = 1 mile
Capacity	cup (c) pint (pt) quart (qt) gallon (gal)	2 cups = 1 pint 2 pints = 1 quart 4 quarts = 1 gallon
Weight	ounce (oz) pound (lb) ton (T)	16 ounces = 1 pound 2,000 pounds = 1 ton

Work with students to fill in the chart entries, as shown above. Then have each student take a turn measuring the length, width, or height of a classroom object. Use things of varied sizes, such as the length of a pencil, the width of a window, the height of a door, etc. Then ask students questions that lead them to use the equivalent measurements. For example, ask *Which is longer, a fence that is 4 feet long, or one that is a yard long?* Repeat until each student has had at least one turn.

Follow a similar procedure with capacity. Have students experiment using water to find the capacity of 1-cup, 2-cup, and 1-quart graduated measuring cups and of a gallon jug. Lead them to understand various equivalent measures.

Finally have each student take a turn using the scale to measure the weight of classroom objects. Have each student share his or her results with the class. Then ask students questions that lead them to use the equivalent measurements. For example, ask *Which is heavier, a stone that weighs 18 ounces, or one that weighs 1 pound?* Repeat until each student has had at least one turn.

Integrating Language

Have students use rulers and the Chapter 24 Worksheet to review and practice what they have learned. You might model the process by working with students to solve the first problem orally. After students have completed their independent work, measure comprehension by checking and discussing their answers.

Name ______________________

Customary Measurement

Measure to the nearest $\frac{1}{4}$ inch.

1. 

$1\frac{3}{4}$ inches

2. 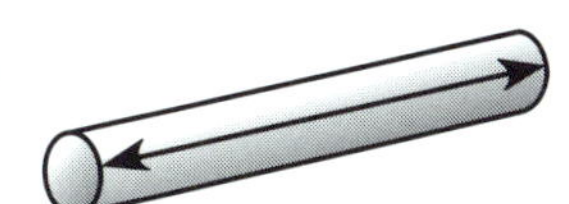

$1\frac{3}{4}$ inches

3. 

$\frac{3}{4}$ inch

Compare the measurements. Write $<$ or $>$.

4. 20 inches ◯ 1 foot, 6 inches $>$

5. 2 cups ◯ 2 pints $<$

6. 25 lb ◯ $\frac{1}{2}$ ton $<$

7. What is the capacity of a container that holds 2 quarts when full? Circle each correct answer.

4 cups   6 cups   (4 pints)   ($\frac{1}{2}$ gallon)

Choose the most reasonable unit of measure. Circle your choice.

8. Weight

oz   (lb)   T

9. Capacity

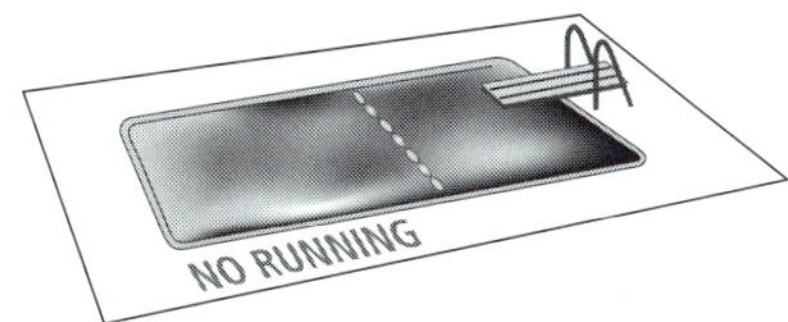

c   qt   (gal)

10. Length

in.   (ft)   mi

Chapter 25

Metric Measurement

Motivation

HANDS-ON REVIEW: Work with students to use a metric ruler, measuring cup, and scale to make linear, capacity, and mass measurements. Use the activity to review the terms *length, width, height, capacity, cup, mass,* as well as the concept of *metric measurements.*

Materials: customary rulers, measuring cup, scale, centimeter rulers, meter stick, milliliter measure, graduated liter measure, tinted water, metric scale (grams/kilograms), road map with key showing distances in miles and kilometers

Concept Vocabulary: ***kilo-, meter (m), liter (l), mass, gram (g)***

On the board, re-create the following chart, containing the vocabulary terms and abbreviations as shown.

The Metric System's Units of Measurements

For this type of measurement:	Use these units:	Equivalents
linear	centimeter (cm) decimeter (dm) meter (m) kilometer (km)	**(1 dm = 10 cm)** **(1 m = 100 cm; 10 dm)** **(1 km = 1,000 m)**
capacity	milliliter (mL) liter (L)	**(1 L = 1,000 mL)**
mass	gram (g) kilogram (kg)	**(1 kg = 1,000 g)**

Display a centimeter ruler and a meter stick. Use them to explain the meaning of *centimeter*, *decimeter*, and *meter*. Then circle the prefix *kilo-* in the term *kilometer*. Point out that this prefix means "one thousand." Therefore, a kilometer equals 1,000 meters. Work with students to fill in the *Equivalents* entries for linear measurement. Use the ruler and meter stick to point out relative lengths.

Display the milliliter and liter measures. Use them to define the capacities of these measures. Work with students to fill in the *Equivalents* section.

Point out the term *mass* on the chart. Define it as the amount of matter in an object. Point out the terms *gram (g)* and *kilogram (kg)*. Ask students to use their knowledge of the prefix *kilo-* to tell how many grams equal one kilogram. Use their answers to fill in the *Equivalents* section.

Guided Instruction

Have each student take a turn using the centimeter ruler and the meter stick to measure the length of classroom objects. Use things of varied lengths, such as a pencil, the width of a window or door, and so on. First, name the object and have the student decide whether to use the ruler or the meter stick. Then have the student measure the object and share his or her results with the class. Use each example as an opportunity to reinforce metric units for measuring length. Then display a road map. Point out the distance, in both miles and kilometers, between various points. Have students use the map and the key to measure other distances in kilometers.

Have students take turns using the milliliter and liter measures to measure the capacity of various bottle caps, glasses, and mugs. Use each example as an opportunity to reinforce metric units for measuring capacity.

Have each student take a turn using the scale to measure the mass of classroom objects. Have each student share his or her results with the class. Use each example as an opportunity to reinforce metric units for measuring mass.

Integrating Language

Have students refer to the metric measuring tools and the chart to answer such questions and riddles as *What are two metric units of mass? What metric unit is the same length as 10 cm? How many grams are in a kilogram? What metric measuring tool would you use to measure this piece of chalk?* Provide each student with as many chances to answer as possible.

Understand Decimals

HANDS-ON REVIEW: Have students use fraction tiles to make models that help them review the concept of a fraction as part of a whole. Then have them make models of mixed numbers to review and reinforce the concept of mixed numbers as numbers that contain whole numbers and fractions.

Materials: fraction tiles, play coins and bills, base-ten blocks, chart paper

Concept Vocabulary: *polygon, perimeter, formula, area, square units*

Write the fraction $\frac{1}{10}$ and the mixed number $1\frac{3}{10}$ on the board. Work with students to use base-ten blocks to build models of each. Have students think of the fraction and mixed number as amounts of money. Use play coins and bills to create models of each. Lead students to understand that $\frac{1}{10}$ of a dollar is $0.10, and $1\frac{3}{10}$ dollars is $1.30. Repeat with other fractions, converting them to amounts of money. Use the exercise to review the use of the decimal point to separate dollars from cents.

Under each amount of money written on the board, write the corresponding decimal. Point out that decimals are like fractions and mixed numbers. They can be part of a whole (less than 1), or a combination of whole numbers and fractions. When they begin with a dollar sign, they stand for amounts of money. When they do not, they stand for fractions and mixed numbers that have a denominator that is a power of 10.

Write the terms *tenths, hundredths,* and *thousandths* on the board and read them aloud. You may wish to circle the *-ths* at the end of each term to allow students to focus on the more familiar words *ten, hundred,* and *thousand*. Then write such decimals as 0.3, 0.03, and 0.003. Use words to read them aloud (three tenths, three hundredths, three thousandths), pointing out the place value of *tenths, hundredths,* and *thousandths*. Stress the position of the decimal point as the separation between a whole number and a fraction. Write such decimals on the board as 1.3, 2.04, and 6.002. Use words to read them aloud.

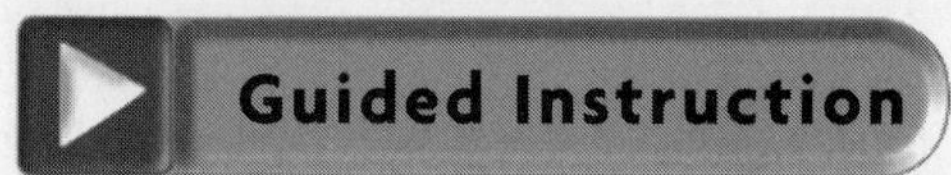

Guided Instruction

On the board or on chart paper, create the following chart:

Ones	Decimal Point	Tenths	Hundredths	Thousandths
	•			
	•			
	•			

Have students take turns. Give each student a decimal to write on the chart. For example, you might say to a student, "Write seven tenths on the chart." Give each student several opportunities to respond, increasing the difficulty as he or she grows more confident.

Then make the following chart:

Standard	Expanded	Word
1.35	**(1 one + 3 tenths + 5 hundredths, OR 1 + 0.3 + 0.05)**	**(one and thirty-five hundredths)**

Model the process of writing a decimal such as 1.35 in standard, expanded, and word forms, as shown above. Then have students take turns making chart entries. For each student, begin by writing a decimal in standard form on the chart. Have the student fill in the expanded and word forms for the decimal. Give each student several opportunities to respond. Begin with such simple decimals as 0.8, and increase difficulty as the students grow more confident.

Integrating Language

Have students work with partners. Give each set of partners a set of base-ten blocks and a list of decimals. Instruct them to keep their assignments secret. Have them build models for their assigned decimals. Check their work for accuracy. Then have sets of partners examine each other's work, naming the decimals that other partners have built, and writing their answers in standard, expanded, and word forms.

Chapter 27

Add and Subtract Decimals

Motivation

ROLE-PLAY: Have volunteers role-play the parts of a customer and a storekeeper. Provide possible prices for several classroom items and have the volunteers role-play a conversation based on the cost of items and any change they might receive from the purchase. For example,
CUSTOMER: I want to buy a pen for 20¢ and a notebook for $1.50.
STOREKEEPER: You owe $1.70.
CUSTOMER: Here is $2.00.
STOREKEEPER: Your change is 30¢.

If necessary, provide play money to help students model the amounts of money. Provide opportunities for several pairs of students to role-play.

Materials: play money, Chapter 27 Worksheet

Concept Vocabulary: ***line up, equivalent decimals***

Write the idiom *line up* on the board and read it aloud. Ask students what they would do if you told them to line up at the door. Elicit that they would form a line, one behind the other. Point out that the same term is used in math when you line up decimal points. As an example, ask students how they would write the following addition problem: Add $1.59 and $0.05. Lead them to understand that the first thing to do is *line up* the decimal points, as shown below.

```
   $1.59
 + $0.05
 -------
```

Draw a loop to emphasize the vertical lining up of the decimal points. Review and emphasize why lining up the decimal point is important.

Write the term *equivalent decimals* on the board and read it aloud. Remind students that *equivalent* means "having equal value," and elicit that *equivalent decimals* have equal values. Provide such examples as 0.8 and 0.80. Have students suggest other examples. Then challenge them to find the equivalent decimals in such groupings as

0.4, 0.04, and 0.40. You may wish to use the activity to review the place values for tenths and hundredths.

Guided Instruction

Reinforce the importance of lining up decimal points and using equivalent decimals when adding and subtracting decimals. Begin by reminding students that adding and subtracting decimals is just like adding and subtracting amounts of money. The only difference is the absence of the dollar sign.

To prove this point, work with students to solve:

\$1.49	1.49
+ \$0.09	+ 0.09

Then use a horizontal format as you write on the board some simple addition and subtraction problems containing decimals, such as: 7.3 + 6.01 = _____ and 8.09 − 0.1 = _____.

Model the process of writing each problem in vertical format, being careful to line up the decimal points. Then model how to use equivalent decimals (7.3 becomes 7.30 and 0.1 becomes 0.10) to solve each problem. Repeat the process, giving each student at least one turn to solve an addition problem and a subtraction problem. As students' confidence grows, increase the difficulty, creating problems that require regrouping. Use the activity to stress the importance of lining up decimal points and using equivalent decimals when adding and subtracting decimals. You might also review the use of rounding and estimating as a way to check whether an answer is reasonable.

Integrating Language

Have students use the Chapter 27 Worksheet to review and practice what they have learned. You might model the process by working with students to solve the first problem orally. After students have completed their independent work, measure comprehension by checking and discussing their answers.

Name ______________________________

Add and Subtract Decimals

In each set of decimals, circle the equivalent decimals.

1. (0.9) (0.90) 0.09 9.9

2. 1.02 (1.20) (1.2) 0.12

3. 3.78 37.08 (3.7) (3.70)

4. (1.5) 1.05 (1.50) 1.55

Find the sums. Be sure to line up the decimal points!

5. 5.05 + 7.09 12.14

6. 0.652 + 1.023 1.675

7. 32.02 + 7.03 39.05

8. 1.25 + 0.89 2.14

Find the differences. Be sure to line up the decimal points!

9. 12.08 − 6.13 5.95

10. 6.22 − 0.46 5.76

11. 0.98 − 0.59 0.39

12. 19.742 − 4.815 14.927

Add or subtract. Use equivalent decimals when necessary.

13. 2.23 + 0.6 2.83

14. 17.32 − 7.045 10.275

15. 2.3 + 0.08 2.38

16. 12 − 0.99 11.01

Add and Subtract Decimals

In each set of decimals, circle the equivalent decimals.

Perimeter of Plane Figures

ACTIVITY: Ask the students to estimate the number of steps they would take to walk around table. Write several estimates on the board. Have a student actually walk around, count the number of steps, and write the number. Have another student use the ruler to measure the distance around and write the number.

Materials: cylinder, strings, foot ruler, Chapter 28 worksheet

Concept Vocabulary: *perimeter, circumference*

Write the word *perimeter* on the board. Tell the students that the distance around a figure is called its perimeter. Lead them to understand that the top of the table is a rectangle and they found the perimeter of that rectangle by estimating, walking, and measuring.

Draw some irregular polygons on the board. Have students find the perimeter of these figures by using a string and then measuring the string using the ruler.

Label the sides of the same polygons with their measurements. Have students demonstrate how they can add the lengths to determine the polygons' perimeters.

Write the word *circumference*. Tell them that the distance around a circle is called the circumference. Have students measure the circumference of the cylinder by estimating and using a string. They can use the ruler to measure the length of the string in inches.

Write the word *diameter*. Review its meaning. Make sure the students know the diameter passes through the center of the circle and has its endpoint on the circle.

Have a student measure the diameter of the cylinder in inches. Have each student divide the circumference (length of string) by the diameter. Make sure the students realize the circumference of a circle is approximately 3 times its diameter.

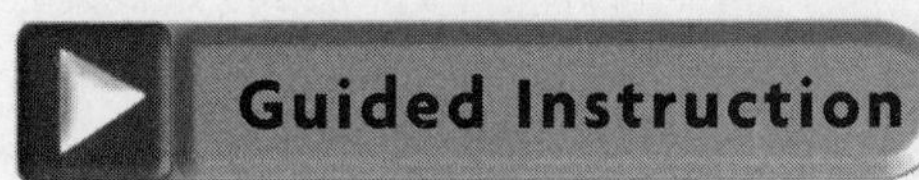

Work with the students to complete this chart.

Perimeter of Regular Polygons		
Name	Side	Perimeter
Triangle	5 cm	$5 + 5 + 5 = 15$ cm
Quadrilateral	5 cm	$5 + 5 + 5 + 5 = 15$ cm
Pentagon	5 cm	$5 + 5 + 5 + 5 + 5 = 25$ cm
Hexagon	5 cm	$5 + 5 + 5 + 5 + 5 + 5 = 30$ cm
Octagon	5 cm	$5 + 5 + 5 + 5 + 5 + 5 + 5 + 5 = 40$ cm

Ask, *Since each side of a regular polygon is the same length, how else could you find the perimeter?* **(multiply the length of a side by the number of sides)**
Describe the quadrilateral in the chart. **(4 equal sides could be a square or rhombus)**
If the perimeter of a square is 36 inches, what is the length of each side? **(36 divided by 4 equals 9; 9 inches)**
What is the circumference of a circle with a diameter of 5 cm? **(about 15 cm)**
If you know the length of a rectangle is 6 inches and its width is 4 inches, how can you find its perimeter?

Have students add each side in order:

length	+	width	+	length	+	width	=	Perimeter
6	+	4	+	6	+	4	=	20 inches

Lead them to see that when they add the length and width twice, they could multiply the sum of the length and width by 2.
Perimeter $= 2\,(l + w)$
Perimeter $= 2(6 + 4) = 2 \times 10 = 20$ inches

Have students add the lengths and then the widths:

length	+	length	+	width	+	length	=	Perimeter
6	+	6	+	4	+	4	=	20 inches

Perimeter $= 2l + 2w$
Perimeter $= 2(2 + 6) + (2 \times 4) = 12 + 8 = 20$ inches

Integrating Language

Have the students complete the Chapter 28 Worksheet by themselves.

Then have the students take turns explaining their answers using the concept vocabulary. You may want them to draw the figures.

Perimeter of Plane Figures

Circle the correct answer.

1. The perimeter of an equilateral triangle with a side 6-cm long is __________.

9 cm   12 cm   18 cm

2. The perimeter of a square is 8 mm. How long is one side?

2 mm   24 mm   32 mm

3. The distance around a polygon is called its __________.

circumference   diameter   perimeter

4. The distance around a circle is called its __________.

circumference   diameter   perimeter

5. The perimeter of a 5-inch by 7-inch rectangle is __________.

12 inches   24 inches   35 inches

6. The circumference of a circle with a diameter of 9 yards is about __________.

3 yards   18 yards   27 yards

7. The perimeter of a regular pentagon is 30 feet. How long is each side?

3 feet   5 feet   6 feet

8. The perimeter of a rectangle is 16 m. Its length is 5 m. What is its width?

3 m   11 m   21 m

9. The circumference of a circle is 12 inches. What is its diameter?

about 4 inches   about 24 inches   about 36 inches

Perimeter of Plane Figures

Circle the correct answer.

1. The perimeter of an equilateral triangle with a side 6 cm long is ______.

9 cm 12 cm 18 cm

2. The perimeter of a square is 8 mm. How long is one side?

3. The distance around a polygon is called its ______.

9. The circumference of a circle is 12 inches. What is its diameter?

about 4 inches about 24 inches about 36 inches

Chapter 29

Area of Plane Figures

Motivation

DISCUSSION: On the chalkboard draw these figures.

4 2 3 3 5 1

Have students take turns naming the length and width of each figure. Discuss the meaning of *perimeter*. Have a student write the formula for perimeter. Then have different students find the perimeters of the figures. (12 units, 12 units, 12 units)
Ask, *If all the figures have perimeters that are the same, why don't they look alike?* **(Each takes up a different amount of space.)**

Materials: different sizes of grid paper for each student, for example, 1-in. grid paper and 1-cm grid paper

Concept Vocabulary: *area*

On the chalkboard write the word *area*.
Say, *When we want to see how much space a figure covers we divide it into square units. We find the area. The area is the number of square units needed to cover a surface. We can either count the squares or we can compute to find the area.*

Have students look at the chalkboard as you draw lines on the figures you drew earlier.

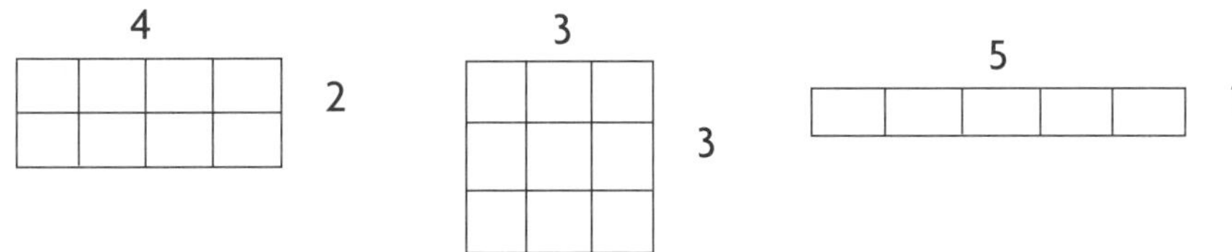

Have a student count the number of squares in the first to find the area. **(8 square units)** Repeat for the other two figures.

Work with the students to use the figures to fill in the table below.

Length	Width	Area
4 units	2 units	**(8 sq. units)**
(3 units)	**(3 units)**	9 sq. units
(5 units)	**(1 unit)**	**(5 sq. units)**

Ask students to examine the length and width of the first figure and to tell what operation they could use to find the area. **(multiplication)** Have them see if this is true of the other two figures.
Lead them to realize that they have found the formula for finding the area of a rectangle: $\mathbf{A = \mathit{l} \times \mathit{w}}$.

Ask:

- *What kind of units do we use to measure length?* **(cm, ft, and so on)**
- *If the first figure is 4 meters long and 2 meters wide, what is its area?* **(8 square meters)**
- *If the second figure is 9 square inches, what is its length and width?* **(3 inches by 3 inches)**
- *Name the dimensions of the third figure in yards.* **(length, 5 yd; width, 1 yd; area, 5 square yards)**
- *Is perimeter measured in units or square units? Why?* **(units, perimeter measures distance around)**
- *What is measured in square units?* **(area)**

Guided Instruction

Give grid paper to each student. Instruct students to draw a rectangle 6 units long and 3 units wide, and to find its perimeter and area. **(P = 18 units; A = 18 square units)**
Have students show their drawings and explain their answers.

Have students draw a rectangle with a length of 7 units and a perimeter of 16 units. Then have them find its width and its area. **(*w* = 1 unit, A = 7 square units)**
Have students show their drawings and explain their answers.

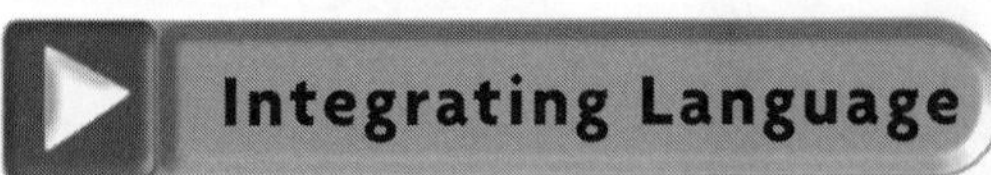

Integrating Language

Write these words on the board: *length, width, area, perimeter, units, square units.*

Have students draw any size rectangle on their grid papers. Then they exchange papers and take turns describing their partner's rectangle using the words above. If they are using 1-cm or 1-in. grid paper have them use the word *centimeter* or *inch* instead of *unit.*

Solid Figures and Volume

HANDS-ON REVIEW: Display the basic geometric solids. To review their knowledge of solid figures, have students take turns identifying each one, and describing its features. Display various plane figures. Have students tell in their own words how plane figures and solid figures are alike and different. If necessary, review the terms *two-dimensional* (having length and width) and *three-dimensional* (having length, width, and height).

Materials: plane figures, basic geometric solids, centimeter ruler, pattern blocks

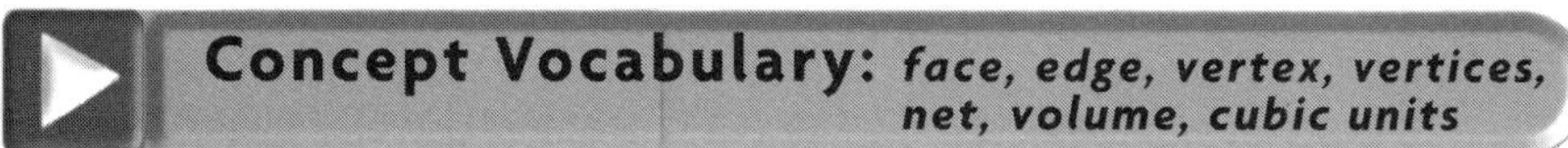

Write the terms *face*, *edge*, *vertex*, and *vertices* on the board and read them aloud. Use a cube as an example, pointing out one face, one edge, and one vertex. Then have students count with you as you count all faces, edges, and vertices. (Make sure that students understand the irregular plural, *vertices*.)

Display a cube and a square. Review their similarities and differences. Write the term *net* on the board and read it aloud. Discuss students' knowledge of its various meanings, pointing out that in math it has a specific and different meaning. Draw on the board, or draw and cut out from paper, a net for a cube. Lead students to understand that a net is a two-dimensional pattern of a three-dimensional figure. Ask students why the net of a cube is made up of six squares, leading them to understand that the six squares represent the six faces of the cube.

Write the terms *volume* and *cubic units* on the board and read them aloud. Again display the square and the cube. Review with students that the area of a square can be computed by multiplying *length* × *width*, and that area is measured in square units. Then draw attention to the cube, and define *volume*. Write the formula *volume* = *length* × *width* × *height* ($V = l \times w \times h$) on the board. Work with students to measure the length, width, and height of the cube. Use the measurements to compute its volume. Emphasize that volume is measured in *cubic units*.

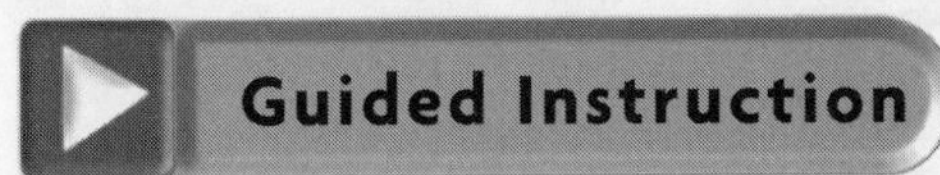

Guided Instruction

On the board, re-create the following chart.

Solid Figure	Number of Faces	Number of Vertices	Number of Edges
cube	**(6)**	**(8)**	**(12)**

Refer students to the net of the cube, and ask them to help you fill in the number of faces, vertices, and edges. Then give each student a geometric solid and ask him or her to tell how many faces, edges, and vertices it has. Have the student create a chart entry to record his or her findings.

Draw or cut from paper nets representing various geometric solids. Have students identify the solid figure that each one represents.

Use pattern blocks to build a 6 cm cube × 4 cm cube × 2 cm cube prism. Ask students to identify the solid figure. Then write the formula $V = l \times w \times h$ on the board. Work with students to compute the volume. (**48 cubic units**) Have them use the term *cubic units* to express the answer. Repeat, having each student build a specific model, use the formula to compute volume, and express the answer in cubic units.

Integrating Language

Play a guessing game. Display the geometric solids. Have students take turns answering riddles such as *I am a solid figure with 5 faces and 6 vertices. What am I?* (**triangular prism**) Have the student select the correct figure from the display. Then ask: *How many edges do I have?* Repeat until each student has had at least one opportunity to respond. Include some riddles about nets as well. Use the activity to reinforce and review the terms *face, vertex, vertices, edge,* and *net*. Then have students work with partners to build large models of rectangular prisms. Have other partners use the formula to compute the volume and express the answer in cubic units. Have model builders check the accuracy of the responses.